What God is Saying in the Book of Revelation

PART 1
DO WE BELIEVE GOD IS AND HIS WORD IS TRUE?

Lorenzo Hill

COPYRIGHT

Copyright © 2020 by Lorenzo Hill.

All rights reserved. No part of this publication may be reproduced, distributed or transmitted in any from or by any means, including photocopying, recording, or other electronic or mechanical methods, without the prior written permission of the publisher, except in the case of brief quotations embodied in critical reviews and certain other noncommercial uses permitted by copyright law.

Scripture quotations taken from the Amplified® Bible (AMP),
Copyright © 2015 by The Lockman Foundation
Used by permission. www.Lockman.org

Scripture quotations taken from the Amplified® Bible (AMPC),
Copyright © 1954, 1958, 1962, 1964, 1965, 1987 by The Lockman Foundation
Used by permission. www.Lockman.org

Scripture Quotations taken from the King James Bible are from Public Domain Version

Book Layout ©2017 BookDesignTemplates.com

What God is Saying in the Book of Revelation; Part 1/ Lorenzo Hill. — 1st ed.
ISBN-13 978-0-9995992-3-5

Table of Contents

COPYRIGHT	II
CHAPTER 1. INTRODUCTION TO THE PROPHECY TO THE SEVEN CHURCHES	1
Summary	13
CHAPTER 2. THE CHURCH JESUS BUILT AT PENTECOST	15
Summary	29
CHAPTER 3. PROPHECY TO THE CHURCH OF EPHESUS	31
Summary	38
CHAPTER 4. PROPHECY TO THE CHURCH IN SMYRNA	41
Summary	50
CHAPTER 5. PROPHECY TO THE CHURCH IN PERGAMOS	57
Summary	64
CHAPTER 6. PROPHECY TO THE CHURCH IN THYATIRA	67
Summary	82
CHAPTER 7. PROPHECY TO THE CHURCH IN SARDIS	85
Summary	88
CHAPTER 8. PROPHECY TO THE CHURCH IN PHILADELPHIA	91
Summary	98
CHAPTER 9. PROPHECY TO THE CHURCH OF THE LAODICEANS	101
Summary	107
CHAPTER 10. JESUS, HIS CLOSING STATEMENT	109
Summary	110
POST SCRIPT	113
APPENDIX	114
SCRIPTURE REFERENCES	115
ABOUT THE AUTHOR	118

Dedicated To
Our Lord and Saviour
Jesus the Christ of Nazareth

REVELATION 1:18-19 KING JAMES VERSION (KJV)

[18] I am he that liveth, and was dead; and, behold, I am alive for evermore, Amen; and have the keys of hell and of death.

[19] Write the things which thou hast seen, and the things which are, and the things which shall be hereafter;

EZEKIEL 12:1-3 AMPLIFIED BIBLE (AMP)

Ezekiel Prepares for Exile

[1] The word of the Lord also came to me, saying,

[2] "Son of man, you live among a rebellious house, who have eyes to see but do not see, who have ears to hear but do not hear; for they are a rebellious people.

[3] Therefore, son of man, prepare your belongings for exile, and move into exile during the day when they will see you; even go into exile from your place to another place as they watch. Perhaps they will understand even though they are a rebellious people.

LUKE 14:34-35 KING JAMES VERSION (KJV)

[34] Salt is good: but if the salt have lost his savour, wherewith shall it be seasoned?

[35] It is neither fit for the land, nor yet for the dunghill; but men cast it out. He that hath ears to hear, let him hear.

LEVITICUS 24:3-4 AMPLIFIED BIBLE (AMP)

[3] Outside the veil of the Testimony [between the Holy Place and the Most Holy Place] in the Tent of Meeting, Aaron shall always keep the lamps [a]burning before the Lord from evening until morning; it shall be a permanent statute throughout your generations.

[4] He shall keep the lamps burning on the pure gold lampstand before the Lord continually.

CHAPTER 1

Introduction to the Prophecy to the Seven Churches

As I laid in bed one night the words which are being placed in this chapter ran through my mind as the Lord related to me the things which we need to learn from the book of Revelation. As He unfolded to me what I was to share with you, we need to realize my heart leaped for joy. You see I have read this scripture many times yet I did not understand its meaning. I have read many interpretations of what the book was saying but none of these satisfied me. In many cases they added to my confusion. Now I was listening to the source and what He wants us to understand by what is written.

One thing we need to realize, based on the way Jesus approached this prophecy, is that He wanted to bring to the forefront in each of us what we are to be concerned with first and foremost in our response to His Spirit, and what we need to be doing in relationship to His Spirit right now. He is presenting what we need to be concerned about today and where we are in relationship to what He requires in the life of the Church. These seven churches are a magnifying glass, showing us the items, that Jesus wants the church to be concerned with. He loves us so much He does not desire for us to fail.

First, I must share a testimony. One day while sitting talking to one of the other ministers in our church, he told me he had an answer for me from the Lord. You see, I had been meditating and trying to digest what was in the book of Revelation. There is so much death and destruction depicted; I just could not accept it. Well, as this minister began speaking, he spoke a word of prophesy to me. He related that the Lord had heard my questions on the book of Revelation. He stated the Lord wanted me to know the answers and that the things written in the book of Revelation are true and they will happen just as they are described. That's when the Lord told me to reread the book. So, I did and as I read it this time, my understanding was opened to the majority of what was in the book. Now I cannot give a time frame for all that is written, but I am called to share those things which have been revealed to me.

Like most of us, I have had a hard time digesting what is written in the book of Revelation. Mostly because it has so many things which I used to consider as symbolic rather than something I could grasp in with my understanding without the necessary inspiration. Again, I also considered it mainly pertained to some future timeframe. My focus has always been on what we in the church needs to know now. My eyes have been opened. Now I ask you to follow along as He provides me with the things, He wishes me to share with you.

So, what is it we need to understand from this prophecy and what is so special about these seven Churches? In the first three chapters, He addresses the seven Churches, pointing out the good and bad which was being demonstrated by their actions. He communicated to each one in very a very concise way why they existed and their role in His plan. Jesus has a plan for His Church to follow. That is why we are told after baptism to seek first the kingdom of God and then all the necessities of life will be added on to you. He is showing us how much He loves us and that He desires for us to succeed.

> **MATTHEW 6:30-34 KING JAMES VERSION (KJV)**
> **[30] Wherefore, if God so clothe the grass of the field, which today is, and to morrow is cast into the oven, shall he not much more clothe you, O ye of little faith?**
> **[31] Therefore take no thought, saying, What shall we eat? or, What shall we drink? or, Wherewithal shall we be clothed?**
> **[32] (For after all these things do the Gentiles seek:) for your heavenly Father knoweth that ye have need of all these things.**
> **[33] But seek ye first the kingdom of God, and his righteousness; and all these things shall be added unto you.**
> **[34] Take therefore no thought for the morrow: for the morrow shall take thought for the things of itself. Sufficient unto the day is the evil thereof.**

In His call to each of the churches He points out the ways the Church was and was not functioning in accordance with the responsibility each Church had. Each one had certain strengths; and some faults which required correction. I asked Him why did He just do this for only these seven Churches? Why not to every group of His followers in each region of the world? From what I am being led to understand, if we study what is being pointed out to each one of these Churches, we find lessons which can be applied universally to each Church in existence, then and now. They are lessons for churches throughout time. When Jesus speaks, He says a lot. His words carry all the weight of the God head and He speaks in eternal terms. Not only is he addressing these seven churches individually, He is speaking to the Church as a whole. That includes us today and those in the future.

He first points to the fact that there is a standard of discipleship expected of us all, and that each one of us is under His scrutiny and is expected to meet certain standards. He is addressing not just seven Churches, but the whole Christian community yesterday, today and tomorrow. These seven Churches had issues which are just as common today as they were 2000 years ago. You see, not a lot has changed.

God has explicit expectations of each of His Churches and if they don't meet them, they will be removed from their place and they will no longer be able to function with His authority. So, let's examine these prophetic instructions as they are presented.

REVELATION 1:10-20 KING JAMES VERSION (KJV)

10 I was in the Spirit on the Lord's day, and heard behind me a great voice, as of a trumpet,

11 Saying, I am Alpha and Omega, the first and the last: and, What thou seest, write in a book, and send it unto the seven Churches which are in Asia; unto Ephesus, and unto Smyrna, and unto Pergamos, and unto Thyatira, and unto Sardis, and unto Philadelphia, and unto Laodicea.

12 And I turned to see the voice that spake with me. And being turned, I saw seven golden candlesticks;

13 And in the midst of the seven candlesticks one like unto the Son of man, clothed with a garment down to the foot, and girt about the paps with a golden girdle.

14 His head and his hairs were white like wool, as white as snow; and his eyes were as a flame of fire;

> [15] *And his feet like unto fine brass, as if they burned in a furnace; and his voice as the sound of many waters.*
> [16] *And he had in his right hand seven stars: and out of his mouth went a sharp twoedged sword: and his countenance was as the sun shineth in his strength.*
> [17] *And when I saw him, I fell at his feet as dead. And he laid his right hand upon me, saying unto me, Fear not; I am the first and the last:*
> [18] *I am he that liveth, and was dead; and, behold, I am alive for evermore, Amen; and have the keys of hell and of death.*
> [19] *Write the things which thou hast seen, and the things which are, and the things which shall be hereafter;*
> [20] *The mystery of the seven stars which thou sawest in my right hand, and the seven golden candlesticks. The seven stars are the angels of the seven Churches: and the seven candlesticks which thou sawest are the seven Churches.*

While John was in the spirit on the Lord's day, Jesus had John put to pen and paper the words of His ongoing plan for man and what will occur in this plan. He started by addressing seven of the existing Churches. He also said, "Blessed is he who reads the words of this prophecy." It is addressed to those of us today and tomorrow, not just those who read the words then. It means those who are being led by the Spirit to really want to understand this prophecy.

I am led to emphasize this one point. That point is John was in the spirit. As I had been meditating on this this the Lord provided me some important insights. There was an experience I had but I have never quite understood. One night the meaning was provided. Just as John, I had experienced what it is meant by the phrase being in the spirit. It is a special state in which the Lord allows us to experience. It is the joining of our spirit and physical being with that which is all around us so that there is no separation between the spiritual and physical universe. John was in such a position. He was one with the Trinity both spiritually and physically much like Jesus was on the Mount of Transfiguration. The two major differences between the experience of John and what I had experienced was that his experience included an angel visitation just as the one on the Mount of Transfiguration. My experience did not include an angelic visitation, nor did I receive a prophesy. Now I can't equate myself with the apostle John or with Jesus at this time, but I know one day I will be like Him as promised in scripture.

1 JOHN 3:1-10 AMPLIFIED BIBLE

Children of God Love One Another

¹ See what an incredible quality of love the Father has shown to us, that we would [be permitted to] be named and called and counted the children of God! And so we are! For this reason the world does not know us, because it did not know Him.

² Beloved, we are [even here and] now children of God, and it is not yet made clear what we will be [after His coming]. We know that when He comes and is revealed, we will [as His children] be like Him, because we will see Him just as He is [in all His glory].

³ And everyone who has this hope [confidently placed] in Him purifies himself, just as He is pure (holy, undefiled, guiltless).

⁴ Everyone who practices sin also practices lawlessness; and sin is lawlessness [ignoring God's law by action or neglect or by tolerating wrongdoing—being unrestrained by His commands and His will].

⁵ You know that He appeared [in visible from as a man] in order to take away sins; and in Him there is [absolutely] no sin [for He has neither the sin nature nor has He committed sin or acts worthy of blame].

⁶ No one who abides in Him [who remains united in fellowship with Him—deliberately, knowingly, and habitually] practices sin. No one who habitually sins has seen Him or known Him.

⁷ Little children (believers, dear ones), do not let anyone lead you astray. The one who practices righteousness [the one who strives to live a consistently honorable life—in private as well as in public—and to confrom to God's precepts] is righteous, just as He is righteous.

⁸ The one who practices sin [separating himself from God, and offending Him by acts of disobedience, indifference, or rebellion] is of the devil [and takes his inner character and moral values from him, not God]; for the devil has sinned and violated God's law from the beginning. The Son of God appeared for this purpose, to destroy the works of the devil.

⁹ No one who is born of God [deliberately, knowingly, and habitually] practices sin, because [a]God's seed [His principle of life, the essence of His righteous character] remains [permanently] in him [who is born again—who is reborn from above—spiritually transformed, renewed, and set apart for His purpose]; and he [who is born again] cannot habitually [live a life characterized by] sin, because he is born of God and longs to please Him.

¹⁰ *By this the children of God and the children of the devil are clearly identified: anyone who does not practice righteousness [who does not seek God's will in thought, action, and purpose] is not of God, nor is the one who does not [unselfishly] [b]love his [believing] brother.*

Footnotes
1 John 3:9 I.e. in human terms, God's seed is like a divine "genetic code" which is passed on to His children and produces in them the desire to live in a way which pleases Him.
1 John 3:10 See note 2:10.
1 John 2:10 The key to understanding this and other statements about love is to know that this love (the Greek word agape) is not so much a matter of emotion as it is of doing things for the benefit of another person, that is, having an unselfish concern for another and a willingness to seek the best for another.

In the first portion of this prophecy we see that there is a leader (represented by the seven stars in His hand) appointed to lead each of the Churches. Jesus represents each Church as a candlestick. He wants us to recall what He taught when He used candlesticks in His teaching in scripture in in relationship to the temple and tabernacle.

EXODUS 30:26-28 KING JAMES VERSION (KJV)
²⁶ *And thou shalt anoint the tabernacle of the congregation therewith, and the ark of the testimony,*
²⁷ *And the table and all his vessels, and the candlestick and his vessels, and the altar of incense,*
²⁸ *And the altar of burnt offering with all his vessels, and the laver and his foot.*

EXODUS 35:13-15 KING JAMES VERSION (KJV)
¹³ *The table, and his staves, and all his vessels, and the shewbread,*
¹⁴ *The candlestick also for the light, and his furniture, and his lamps, with the oil for the light,*
¹⁵ *And the incense altar, and his staves, and the anointing oil, and the sweet incense, and the hanging for the door at the entering in of the tabernacle,*

LEVITICUS 24:3-4 AMPLIFIED BIBLE (AMP)
³ *Outside the veil of the Testimony [between the Holy Place and the Most Holy Place] in the Tent of Meeting, Aaron shall always keep the lamps [a]burning before the Lord from evening until morning; it shall be a permanent statute throughout your generations.*
⁴ *He shall keep the lamps burning on the pure gold lampstand before the Lord continually.*

Footnotes:
Leviticus 24:3 Lit it in order.

MATTHEW 5:14-16 KING JAMES VERSION (KJV)
[14] Ye are the light of the world. A city that is set on an hill cannot be hid.
[15] Neither do men light a candle, and put it under a bushel, but on a candlestick; and it giveth light unto all that are in the house.
[16] Let your light so shine before men, that they may see your good works, and glorify your Father which is in heaven.

You can see here that Jesus' intent in describing the churches as candlesticks starts with the use of the candlestick in the Sanctuary. The candlestick is made to bring light into the darkness. Darkness in scripture refers to the condition of being without God and the light the candle produces overcomes the darkness and sheds forth the work of God. These candlesticks do not use wax candles. They are the type which use oil as fuel to keep the wick burning.

In the description of the candlesticks in the Sanctuary, we are told that special oil is required. This oil was a made and prepared using distinct elements and procedures as dictated by God. In this image the oil is pure, the same as in the temple. Preparation of this required specific steps to be performed. Oil is representative of several things. One is the Holy Spirit. Then there is scripture. Then there is the priesthood. The oil for the temple lamps was prepared by the people. No ordinary oil would do. Only a pure oil is to be used. The oil for the lamps was to be pure and set apart as Holy. In the old testament id describes the procedures needed to prepare this oil. Here we can see that the people had a vital role in the making sure the oil was as instructed. Then, the priests were men whose function was to keep the lamps burning. The priests had to wear special garments to minster. The garments represented the Holy Spirit and Jesus' role in their ministry. These three - the people, the priests, and scripture – were all required to provide proper fuel to keep the wick burning so light can be produced. Here, I am led to interject this. In many places in scripture we are portrayed as a temple. From this we are to understand that the candlestick not only provides light to the outside world, it also represents the preparation necessary to have proper light produced. At work here in this image, is the Churches who are a vital part in producing the light and the oil or fuel, which is the Holy Spirit, and the priesthood which is to keep the lampstand full of fuel so that light can be produced. The duty of the Church is to bring forth the work of God (the light produced by the pure oil) in a world without Him and to bring to the forefront the work of God within (the inner light).

EXODUS 27:19-21 AMPLIFIED BIBLE
19 All the tabernacle's utensils and instruments used in all its service, and all its stakes, and all the stakes for the court, shall be of bronze.
20 "You shall command the Israelites to provide you with clear oil of beaten olives for the light, to make a lamp burn continually [every night].
21 In the Tent of Meeting [of God with His people], outside the veil which is in front of the [ark of the] Testimony [and sets it apart], Aaron [the high priest] and his sons shall keep the lamp burning from evening to morning before the Lord. It shall be a perpetual statute [to be observed] throughout their generations on behalf of the Israelites.

MATTHEW 25:2-10 KING JAMES VERSION (KJV)
2 And five of them were wise, and five were foolish.
3 They that were foolish took their lamps, and took no oil with them:
4 But the wise took oil in their vessels with their lamps.
5 While the bridegroom tarried, they all slumbered and slept.
6 And at midnight there was a cry made, Behold, the bridegroom cometh; go ye out to meet him.
7 Then all those virgins arose, and trimmed their lamps.
8 And the foolish said unto the wise, Give us of your oil; for our lamps are gone out.
9 But the wise answered, saying, Not so; lest there be not enough for us and you: but go ye rather to them that sell, and buy for yourselves.
10 And while they went to buy, the bridegroom came; and they that were ready went in with him to the marriage: and the door was shut.

He also uses the image of the priesthood to keeping the candles supplied with fuel so that they continually provide light on the items in the temple which were representations of His sacrificial love for each of us. This is the same as when He points to the angels who were in charge of the Churches. That is the angels who were in charge are those who are called to look after the spiritual welfare of the churches. Their responsibility is to receive the counsel of Christ and they are to pass this counsel for direction the churches to keep them in the light of His gospel and to point them in the right direction.

One thing to understand is that the image of the stars in His hand represents that He is the source of authority of these angels. These angels are under His control and receive their power and all that they are called to do from Him. Angels are His messengers and their responsibility are to be faithful deliverers of His messages. Along with God's heavenly angels, God appoints individuals as messengers here on earth such as the judges, whose responsibility it was to keep Israel on the right path and lead them in battle against earthly enemies. The earthly leaders are indicated by the fact the prophecies were written down to be delivered in this manner. These angels, who were the watchmen on the wall, are to be ready to receive God's call to guide the people and to warn and prepare for the impending attack of the enemy. Note, these messengers are men and women called by God not by their choice but by their agreement to serve Him. He appoints some as prophets, who are His earthly messengers. Their role is to also provide direct guidance from God. Yet there is a difference between an angel and a prophet. An angel will always deliver the message required without question or debate but a prophet may not. A prophet has human limitations whereas an angel does not. An angel has no fear, his understanding, trust and allegiance to Christ is far superior than that of man. Yet man can achieve this status if he is faithful to the work of the Holy Spirit.

1 CORINTHIANS 12:27-29 KING JAMES VERSION (KJV)
²⁷ Now ye are the body of Christ, and members in particular.
²⁸ And God hath set some in the Church, first apostles, secondarily prophets, thirdly teachers, after that miracles, then gifts of healings, helps, governments, diversities of tongues.
²⁹ Are all apostles? are all prophets? are all teachers? are all workers of miracles?
1 TIMOTHY 3:1-15 KING JAMES VERSION (KJV)
3 This is a true saying, if a man desire the office of a bishop, he desireth a good work.
² A bishop then must be blameless, the husband of one wife, vigilant, sober, of good behaviour, given to hospitality, apt to teach;
³ Not given to wine, no striker, not greedy of filthy lucre; but patient, not a brawler, not covetous;

⁴ One that ruleth well his own house, having his children in subjection with all gravity;
⁵ (For if a man know not how to rule his own house, how shall he take care of the Church of God?)
⁶ Not a novice, lest being lifted up with pride he fall into the condemnation of the devil.
⁷ Moreover he must have a good report of them which are without; lest he fall into reproach and the snare of the devil.
⁸ Likewise must the deacons be grave, not doubletongued, not given to much wine, not greedy of filthy lucre;
⁹ Holding the mystery of the faith in a pure conscience.
¹⁰ And let these also first be proved; then let them use the office of a deacon, being found blameless.
¹¹ Even so must their wives be grave, not slanderers, sober, faithful in all things.
¹² Let the deacons be the husbands of one wife, ruling their children and their own houses well.
¹³ For they that have used the office of a deacon well purchase to themselves a good degree, and great boldness in the faith which is in Christ Jesus.
¹⁴ These things write I unto thee, hoping to come unto thee shortly:
¹⁵ But if I tarry long, that thou mayest know how thou oughtest to behave thyself in the house of God, which is the Church of the living God, the pillar and ground of the truth.

EPHESIANS 4:1-30 KING JAMES VERSION (KJV)

⁴ I therefore, the prisoner of the Lord, beseech you that ye walk worthy of the vocation wherewith ye are called,
² With all lowliness and meekness, with longsuffering, forbearing one another in love;
³ Endeavouring to keep the unity of the Spirit in the bond of peace.
⁴ There is one body, and one Spirit, even as ye are called in one hope of your calling;
⁵ One Lord, one faith, one baptism,
⁶ One God and Father of all, who is above all, and through all, and in you all.
⁷ But unto every one of us is given grace according to the measure of the gift of Christ.
⁸ Wherefore he saith, When he ascended up on high, he led captivity captive, and gave gifts unto men.
⁹ (Now that he ascended, what is it but that he also descended first into the lower parts of the earth?

¹⁰ He that descended is the same also that ascended up far above all heavens, that he might fill all things.)

¹¹ And he gave some, apostles; and some, prophets; and some, evangelists; and some, pastors and teachers;

¹² For the perfecting of the saints, for the work of the ministry, for the edifying of the body of Christ:

¹³ Till we all come in the unity of the faith, and of the knowledge of the Son of God, unto a perfect man, unto the measure of the stature of the fulness of Christ:

¹⁴ That we henceforth be no more children, tossed to and fro, and carried about with every wind of doctrine, by the sleight of men, and cunning craftiness, whereby they lie in wait to deceive;

¹⁵ But speaking the truth in love, may grow up into him in all things, which is the head, even Christ:

¹⁶ From whom the whole body fitly joined together and compacted by that which every joint supplieth, according to the effectual working in the measure of every part, maketh increase of the body unto the edifying of itself in love.

¹⁷ This I say therefore, and testify in the Lord, that ye henceforth walk not as other Gentiles walk, in the vanity of their mind,

¹⁸ Having the understanding darkened, being alienated from the life of God through the ignorance that is in them, because of the blindness of their heart:

¹⁹ Who being past feeling have given themselves over unto lasciviousness, to work all uncleanness with greediness.

²⁰ But ye have not so learned Christ;

²¹ If so be that ye have heard him, and have been taught by him, as the truth is in Jesus:

²² That ye put off concerning the fromer conversation the old man, which is corrupt according to the deceitful lusts;

²³ And be renewed in the spirit of your mind;

²⁴ And that ye put on the new man, which after God is created in righteousness and true holiness.

²⁵ Wherefore putting away lying, speak every man truth with his neighbour: for we are members one of another.

²⁶ Be ye angry, and sin not: let not the sun go down upon your wrath:

²⁷ Neither give place to the devil.

²⁸ Let him that stole steal no more: but rather let him labour, working with his hands the thing which is good, that he may have to give to him that needeth.

> *²⁹ Let no corrupt communication proceed out of your mouth, but that which is good to the use of edifying, that it may minister grace unto the hearers.*
> *³⁰ And grieve not the holy Spirit of God, whereby ye are sealed unto the day of redemption.*

Next is the fact that we in the Church are called to demonstrate to the upmost in all we do, His righteousness and love. We are called to perform all things for the glory of God. We are to honor the call to renounce our past sinful practices and allow Him to place in us the new life, which is in His image. We have the call to separate ourselves from worldly works by our commitment to Him. We are to do all to glorify Him and not just seek the good life. If we allow Him to perform this work, all things will become new and we will love as He loves. We will do all things in the similitude of His love. We are to be pure and holy just as the oil in the lamp. We have to prepare to supply the pure oil, so the light is produced by following His righteous works. Without a pure and God like commitment, we are just ordinary and common place.

> **ACTS 2:38-40 KING JAMES VERSION (KJV)**
> *³⁸ Then Peter said unto them, Repent, and be baptized every one of you in the name of Jesus Christ for the remission of sins, and ye shall receive the gift of the Holy Ghost.*
> *³⁹ For the promise is unto you, and to your children, and to all that are afar off, even as many as the Lord our God shall call.*
> *⁴⁰ And with many other words did he testify and exhort, saying, Save yourselves from this untoward generation.*

The act of saving ourselves is the acceptance of Jesus as our Saviour and adherence to His commandments. Salvation is His to give and ours to receive. Without true repentance and true acceptance of Him as savior and the regenerated lifestyle imparted through the Holy Spirit, we are not of Him, but are still in the world. This message is repeated over and over in the prophecies supplied to the seven Churches. The plan of Christ is to have a Church without spot or blemish to present before God. If we are truly His, we are reborn in His image.

> **EPHESIANS 5:26-28 AMPLIFIED BIBLE**
> *²⁶ so that He might sanctify the Church, having cleansed her by the washing of water with the word [of God],*
> *²⁷ so that [in turn] He might present the Church to Himself in glorious splendor, without spot or wrinkle or any such thing; but that she would be holy [set apart for God] and blameless.*

²⁸ Even so husbands should and are morally obligated to love their own wives as [being in a sense] their own bodies. He who loves his own wife loves himself.

Summary

Here is the introduction of the prophecy to the seven Churches. It is being presented by a heavenly messenger to one of His earthly messengers under the authority of Jesus the Christ. This fits with the image of the seven stars who are the angels of the seven Churches. The leaders are both heavenly and earthly. Both are under His authority, appointed and chosen by Him.

So, what are we to gain from this?
1. Jesus has a plan for His Church.
2. Each Church is being constantly evaluated by Him.
3. The message is being presented by loyal, chosen, authoritative servants whom He can trust to deliver it as it is presented.
4. He loves us enough that He, Himself, is the one providing these evaluations and He is here to support us in the Church.
5. The image of Jesus provides insights to characteristics which He wants the Churches to understand. As in the parables, the images are presented in a from which only those who are attuned to Him will understand.
    a. His wisdom is represented by age, i.e., His white hair and countenance.
    b. The dividing of truth from falsehood by the two-edged sword for a tongue, is in the power of His word to distinguish between the two.
    c. The sash represents His authority as ruler.
    d. The white robe exemplifies His purity.
    e. Feet of burnished brass which exemplifies Him as a firm foundation, untarnished, without dirt on them. In the temple, the stakes which held supported the temple were made of brass.

6. It takes one with a willing heart to receive what He is stating. This is a message to those who are willing to know and understand its meaning. We can take it or leave it.
7. Not everyone will have the will or interest in receiving the message He is giving.
8. Golden candlesticks symbolize that the reason for existence of the Church is to provide, after conversion, light in a sinful world.
9. Note also that the candlesticks are stands which places them so the light is above the sinful world and can be seen from all directions and for a greater distance.
10. Each lamp needs the oil to keep burning. The oil is provided by the works of the saints living in accordance with Jesus' commandments. These are to be prepared by a pure and holy people powered by a regenerated life and the power of the Holy Spirit to magnify Christ to the world.
11. It is the duty of the priesthood to keep oil in the lamps and to represent Christ to the church, keeping them informed of His words so they can perform the good works ordained by God.

CHAPTER 2

The Church Jesus Built at Pentecost

The spirit pointed me to the description of the early Church in the book of Acts. I am led to believe that those who were transformed on the day of Pentecost were the ones who were demonstrating the correct traits of what it means to be made anew in the image of Christ. We need to compare what was so special about this group and how that translates into the prophecy provided to the seven Churches. Let's examine their predominant features. First and foremost, there was a phenomenal move of the Holy Spirit on the day of Pentecost. All those around heard the proclamation of Jesus as Saviour in their own tongue so there was no mistaking what they heard. They heard in perfect word usage and inflection in a way that the meaning of the message needed no interpretation - just as the Lord speaks to me. He doesn't use proper English or Elizabethan English but with phrases and terminology that I understand. Not all who heard responded, but those that did respond were instantly transformed from their old selves as they were baptized into the basic image of Christ. There was more they needed to learn but the most important attributes were provided on that day, to trust and love God and love their neighbor as well as themselves. Many of these had been witnessed to by those who were released from their graves after the resurrection of Jesus. So, they understood the reality of eternal life and they had received the proof of its existence. Now let's review how this was expressed in the way they approached their new life in Christ.

One form of expression the act of adding to the Church daily. This evidences that they were fervently spreading the good news. They were preaching repentance and belief in Christ Jesus, Him crucified and Him raised from the dead. This included receipt of forgiveness of sin, the gift of eternal life, and the receipt of the gift of the Comforter and His revitalization of their spiritual and physical nature. They taught that true repentance included confessing their sins and that they had not recognized and glorified God in their lifestyle, followed the principles of loving God with all their heart mind and strength or loving their neighbor as themselves. Note that I am not listing each way they could sin but used the expression Jesus did which included the way man can overcome sin and live out the perfect way in which we are created to live. Those who were willing received the work of the Holy Spirit which changed their way of thinking and doing things. They practiced what Jesus preached. You can find this in the message delivered by Peter on the day of Pentecost. They performed miracles by the power and faith provided by the Holy Spirit as evidence that God was with them. They met together daily studying scripture. They allowed the Holy Spirit to change their attitude about everything including that of property. They realized that none of it was theirs so they shared their wealth freely with one another. Tithing was no longer the accepted standard. They wanted everyone in the fellowship to have their needs met because they now loved their brothers and sisters just as God does. Loving God and each other in a Godly manner were the reasons behind everything they did. They no longer saw the need to hoard possession. They shared meals together daily as they studied scripture. They also sold excess property and they put the proceeds in the hands of the elders to distribute to those who had need. They had a gift the Holy Spirit who provided a true understanding of what was God was saying in scripture. They were now able to see the true meaning of scripture unlike the interpretations provided by biblical scholars. There was a new level of aptitude and a new desire for understanding the love of God portrayed in the scripture. They were living a kingdom lifestyle.

A new attitude prevailed. This was demonstrated by the fact they no longer desired to hoard things for themselves because they understood that God had provided everything+ for the benefit of all mankind not just a few. He has provided enough for us all if we share equitably, not just in possessions but in His good works.

ACTS 2:2-47 KING JAMES VERSION (KJV)

² And suddenly there came a sound from heaven as of a rushing mighty wind, and it filled all the house where they were sitting.

³ And there appeared unto them cloven tongues like as of fire, and it sat upon each of them.

⁴ And they were all filled with the Holy Ghost, and began to speak with other tongues, as the Spirit gave them utterance.

⁵ And there were dwelling at Jerusalem Jews, devout men, out of every nation under heaven.

⁶ Now when this was noised abroad, the multitude came together, and were confounded, because that every man heard them speak in his own language.

⁷ And they were all amazed and marvelled, saying one to another, Behold, are not all these which speak Galilaeans?

⁸ And how hear we every man in our own tongue, wherein we were born?

⁹ Parthians, and Medes, and Elamites, and the dwellers in Mesopotamia, and in Judaea, and Cappadocia, in Pontus, and Asia,

¹⁰ Phrygia, and Pamphylia, in Egypt, and in the parts of Libya about Cyrene, and strangers of Rome, Jews and proselytes,

¹¹ Cretes and Arabians, we do hear them speak in our tongues the wonderful works of God.

¹² And they were all amazed, and were in doubt, saying one to another, What meaneth this?

¹³ Others mocking said, These men are full of new wine.

¹⁴ But Peter, standing up with the eleven, lifted up his voice, and said unto them, Ye men of Judaea, and all ye that dwell at Jerusalem, be this known unto you, and hearken to my words:

¹⁵ For these are not drunken, as ye suppose, seeing it is but the third hour of the day.

¹⁶ But this is that which was spoken by the prophet Joel;

¹⁷ And it shall come to pass in the last days, saith God, I will pour out of my Spirit upon all flesh: and your sons and your daughters shall prophesy, and your young men shall see visions, and your old men shall dream dreams:

¹⁸ And on my servants and on my handmaidens I will pour out in those days of my Spirit; and they shall prophesy:

¹⁹ And I will shew wonders in heaven above, and signs in the earth beneath; blood, and fire, and vapour of smoke:
²⁰ The sun shall be turned into darkness, and the moon into blood, before the great and notable day of the Lord come:
²¹ And it shall come to pass, that whosoever shall call on the name of the Lord shall be saved.
²² Ye men of Israel, hear these words; Jesus of Nazareth, a man approved of God among you by miracles and wonders and signs, which God did by him in the midst of you, as ye yourselves also know:
²³ Him, being delivered by the determinate counsel and foreknowledge of God, ye have taken, and by wicked hands have crucified and slain:
²⁴ Whom God hath raised up, having loosed the pains of death: because it was not possible that he should be holden of it.
²⁵ For David speaketh concerning him, I foresaw the Lord always before my face, for he is on my right hand, that I should not be moved:
²⁶ Therefore did my heart rejoice, and my tongue was glad; moreover also my flesh shall rest in hope:
²⁷ Because thou wilt not leave my soul in hell, neither wilt thou suffer thine Holy One to see corruption.
²⁸ Thou hast made known to me the ways of life; thou shalt make me full of joy with thy countenance.
²⁹ Men and brethren, let me freely speak unto you of the patriarch David, that he is both dead and buried, and his sepulchre is with us unto this day.
³⁰ Therefore being a prophet, and knowing that God had sworn with an oath to him, that of the fruit of his loins, according to the flesh, he would raise up Christ to sit on his throne;
³¹ He seeing this before spake of the resurrection of Christ, that his soul was not left in hell, neither his flesh did see corruption.
³² This Jesus hath God raised up, whereof we all are witnesses.
³³ Therefore being by the right hand of God exalted, and having received of the Father the promise of the Holy Ghost, he hath shed forth this, which ye now see and hear.
³⁴ For David is not ascended into the heavens: but he saith himself, The Lord said unto my Lord, Sit thou on my right hand,
³⁵ Until I make thy foes thy footstool.
³⁶ Therefore let all the house of Israel know assuredly, that God hath made the same Jesus, whom ye have crucified, both Lord and Christ.

37 Now when they heard this, they were pricked in their heart, and said unto Peter and to the rest of the apostles, Men and brethren, what shall we do?
38 Then Peter said unto them, Repent, and be baptized every one of you in the name of Jesus Christ for the remission of sins, and ye shall receive the gift of the Holy Ghost.
39 For the promise is unto you, and to your children, and to all that are afar off, even as many as the Lord our God shall call.
40 And with many other words did he testify and exhort, saying, Save yourselves from this untoward generation.
41 Then they that gladly received his word were baptized: and the same day there were added unto them about three thousand souls.
42 And they continued stedfastly in the apostles' doctrine and fellowship, and in breaking of bread, and in prayers.
43 And fear came upon every soul: and many wonders and signs were done by the apostles.
44 And all that believed were together, and had all things common;
45 And sold their possessions and goods, and parted them to all men, as every man had need.
46 And they, continuing daily with one accord in the temple, and breaking bread from house to house, did eat their meat with gladness and singleness of heart,
47 Praising God, and having favour with all the people. And the Lord added to the Church daily such as should be saved.

Yes, they were equipped to battle the evil challenges (which are also spiritual) of the day but also to resist the elements of false doctrine being introduced by false teachers and disciples of the devil. Those who were sent to disrupt the work of Jesus Christ. They were demonstrating the true intent of the law of God and the reason for His creation of man. They accepted all who had received the baptism of the Holy Spirit as brothers and sisters in Christ. No longer were there divisions based on nationality, race, sex, education, wealth, or status. They accepted we are all created equal in the eyes of God. They understood and lived as it is in heaven. They had been converted from a life filled with ideas of one person being better than another. They were all one in Christ Jesus and one family in God. No one was esteemed above another and no one was less than any other. Truly the kingdom being lived out on earth.

> **GALATIANS 3:27-29 AMPLIFIED BIBLE (AMP)**
> **²⁷** *For all of you who were baptized into Christ [into a spiritual union with the Christ, the Anointed] have clothed yourselves with Christ [that is, you have taken on His characteristics and values].*
> **²⁸** *There is [now no distinction in regard to salvation] neither Jew nor Greek, there is neither slave nor free, there is neither male nor female; for you [who believe] are all one in Christ Jesus [no one can claim a spiritual superiority].*
> **²⁹** *And if you belong to Christ [if you are in Him], then you are Abraham's descendants, and [spiritual] heirs according to [God's] promise.*

Yes, there were those who falsely claimed belief in Christ and were only there for what they could gain from the generosity of the saints; free food, clothes and money, an easy life style. They worked in two realms. One was the spiritual and one was the flesh. Through the power of the Holy Spirit they were able to have victory over the flesh and live a life governed by the righteousness of God. As the ranks of the group swelled many came in who had not yielded to the conversion work of the Holy Spirit. As a result, there were admonitions to treat these as infections and cast them from the body until they repented.

> **1 CORINTHIANS 2:14-16 AMPLIFIED BIBLE (AMP)**
> **¹⁴** *But the natural [unbelieving] man does not accept the things [the teachings and revelations] of the Spirit of God, for they are foolishness [absurd and illogical] to him; and he is incapable of understanding them, because they are spiritually discerned and appreciated, [and he is unqualified to judge spiritual matters].*
> **¹⁵** *But the spiritual man [the spiritually mature Christian] judges all things [questions, examines and applies what the Holy Spirit reveals], yet is himself judged by no one [the unbeliever cannot judge and understand the believer's spiritual nature].*
> **¹⁶** *For who has known the mind and purposes of the Lord, so as to instruct Him? But we have the mind of Christ [to be guided by His thoughts and purposes].*

> **1 CORINTHIANS 5:12-13 AMPLIFIED BIBLE (AMP)**
> **¹²** *For what business is it of mine to judge outsiders (non-believers)? Do you not judge those who are within the Church [to protect the Church as the situation requires]?*
> **¹³** *God alone sits in judgment on those who are outside [the faith]. Remove the wicked one from among you [expel him from your Church].*

Another attribute is the way they approached worship. They all came prepared. Worship was communal. Each individual came prepared to offer what the Lord had placed on their hearts. For one it might be the reading and commenting on a certain scripture. For another it was the sharing of a song, for another it might be sharing a word of prophesy, for another it might be an offer of praise in prayer. Each one of the truly reborn Christians had been praying and were guided by the Holy Spirit as to how they were to contribute. Because we to today have strayed away from this style of worship we have adopted a style which has crept into the church. There is only a limited group controlling what is being presented. The rest are left to sit and be quiet, we are spiritually inept. We have accepted a standard which was fostered by corruption and cultural allegiances as our guide rather than the way God wants these things to be done. Even in synagogues of the day they would offer those who were willing to read scripture just as Jesus did when He read from the book of Isiah.

1 CORINTHIANS 14:20-33 KING JAMES VERSION (KJV)

[20] Brethren, be not children in understanding: howbeit in malice be ye children, but in understanding be men.

[21] In the law it is written, With men of other tongues and other lips will I speak unto this people; and yet for all that will they not hear me, saith the Lord.

[22] Wherefore tongues are for a sign, not to them that believe, but to them that believe not: but prophesying serveth not for them that believe not, but for them which believe.

[23] If therefore the whole Church be come together into one place, and all speak with tongues, and there come in those that are unlearned, or unbelievers, will they not say that ye are mad?

[24] But if all prophesy, and there come in one that believeth not, or one unlearned, he is convinced of all, he is judged of all:

[25] And thus are the secrets of his heart made manifest; and so falling down on his face he will worship God, and report that God is in you of a truth.

[26] How is it then, brethren? when ye come together, every one of you hath a psalm, hath a doctrine, hath a tongue, hath a revelation, hath an interpretation. Let all things be done unto edifying.

[27] If any man speak in an unknown tongue, let it be by two, or at the most by three, and that by course; and let one interpret.

[28] But if there be no interpreter, let him keep silence in the Church; and let him speak to himself, and to God.

²⁹ *Let the prophets speak two or three, and let the other judge.*
³⁰ *If any thing be revealed to another that sitteth by, let the first hold his peace.*
³¹ *For ye may all prophesy one by one, that all may learn, and all may be comforted.*
³² *And the spirits of the prophets are subject to the prophets.*
³³ *For God is not the author of confusion, but of peace, as in all Churches of the saints.*

LUKE 4:14-21 KING JAMES VERSION (KJV)

¹⁴ *And Jesus returned in the power of the Spirit into Galilee: and there went out a fame of him through all the region round about.*
¹⁵ *And he taught in their synagogues, being glorified of all.*
¹⁶ *And he came to Nazareth, where he had been brought up: and, as his custom was, he went into the synagogue on the sabbath day, and stood up for to read.*
¹⁷ *And there was delivered unto him the book of the prophet Esaias. And when he had opened the book, he found the place where it was written,*
¹⁸ *The Spirit of the Lord is upon me, because he hath anointed me to preach the gospel to the poor; he hath sent me to heal the brokenhearted, to preach deliverance to the captives, and recovering of sight to the blind, to set at liberty them that are bruised,*
¹⁹ *To preach the acceptable year of the Lord.*
²⁰ *And he closed the book, and he gave it again to the minister, and sat down. And the eyes of all them that were in the synagogue were fastened on him.*
²¹ *And he began to say unto them, This day is this scripture fulfilled in your ears.*

Now, this is the biggie. They no longer feared death because they were assured of eternal life. Death is the greatest fear in most of us. We don't seem to grasp the truth of eternal life. It is not a ploy to trick you. It is a reality.

Jesus was the first to achieve eternal life. After Him were those who rose from the grave immediately after His resurrection. They went into the cities and witnessed to many. This is a point of contention in the modern western church. Many try to explain this away as folklore or as an imaginary idea or a fable or something invented by ignorant people. Those who truly believed this even going back into the Old Testament would face perils with heartfelt ease knowing that this was true. Paul makes a profound statement in which he emphasizes: if eternal life is not true, then all that we accept about Jesus and the new life is worthless and we might as well do what brings us pleasure and forget the gospel. He brings this to a head and lays it firmly on the line. If the promise of eternal life is not true nothing we have heard or what we hear about Christ is true therefore why waste your time. He states this is the essence of all we are as Christians. Here is this statement in scripture.

1 CORINTHIANS 15:10-25 KING JAMES VERSION (KJV)

[10] But by the grace of God I am what I am: and his grace which was bestowed upon me was not in vain; but I laboured more abundantly than they all: yet not I, but the grace of God which was with me.

[11] Therefore whether it were I or they, so we preach, and so ye believed.

[12] Now if Christ be preached that he rose from the dead, how say some among you that there is no resurrection of the dead?

[13] But if there be no resurrection of the dead, then is Christ not risen:

[14] And if Christ be not risen, then is our preaching vain, and your faith is also vain.

[15] Yea, and we are found false witnesses of God; because we have testified of God that he raised up Christ: whom he raised not up, if so be that the dead rise not.

[16] For if the dead rise not, then is not Christ raised:

[17] And if Christ be not raised, your faith is vain; ye are yet in your sins.

[18] Then they also which are fallen asleep in Christ are perished.

[19] If in this life only we have hope in Christ, we are of all men most miserable.

[20] But now is Christ risen from the dead, and become the firstfruits of them that slept.

[21] For since by man came death, by man came also the resurrection of the dead.

[22] For as in Adam all die, even so in Christ shall all be made alive.

[23] But every man in his own order: Christ the firstfruits; afterward they that are Christ's at his coming.

[24] Then cometh the end, when he shall have delivered up the kingdom to God, even the Father; when he shall have put down all rule and all authority and power.

[25] For he must reign, till he hath put all enemies under his feet.

1 CORINTHIANS 15:31-50 KING JAMES VERSION (KJV)

[31] I protest by your rejoicing which I have in Christ Jesus our Lord, I die daily.

³² If after the manner of men I have fought with beasts at Ephesus, what advantageth it me, if the dead rise not? let us eat and drink; for to morrow we die.
³³ Be not deceived: evil communications corrupt good manners.
³⁴ Awake to righteousness, and sin not; for some have not the knowledge of God: I speak this to your shame.
³⁵ But some man will say, How are the dead raised up? and with what body do they come?
³⁶ Thou fool, that which thou sowest is not quickened, except it die:
³⁷ And that which thou sowest, thou sowest not that body that shall be, but bare grain, it may chance of wheat, or of some other grain:
³⁸ But God giveth it a body as it hath pleased him, and to every seed his own body.
³⁹ All flesh is not the same flesh: but there is one kind of flesh of men, another flesh of beasts, another of fishes, and another of birds.
⁴⁰ There are also celestial bodies, and bodies terrestrial: but the glory of the celestial is one, and the glory of the terrestrial is another.
⁴¹ There is one glory of the sun, and another glory of the moon, and another glory of the stars: for one star differeth from another star in glory.
⁴² So also is the resurrection of the dead. It is sown in corruption; it is raised in incorruption:
⁴³ It is sown in dishonour; it is raised in glory: it is sown in weakness; it is raised in power:
⁴⁴ It is sown a natural body; it is raised a spiritual body. There is a natural body, and there is a spiritual body.
⁴⁵ And so it is written, The first man Adam was made a living soul; the last Adam was made a quickening spirit.
⁴⁶ Howbeit that was not first which is spiritual, but that which is natural; and afterward that which is spiritual.
⁴⁷ The first man is of the earth, earthy; the second man is the Lord from heaven.
⁴⁸ As is the earthy, such are they also that are earthy: and as is the heavenly, such are they also that are heavenly.
⁴⁹ And as we have borne the image of the earthy, we shall also bear the image of the heavenly.
⁵⁰ Now this I say, brethren, that flesh and blood cannot inherit the kingdom of God; neither doth corruption inherit incorruption.

Those transformed on the day of Pentecost, had received the conformation of this truth and were willing to face anything, even some of the most horrible deaths, rather than denounce Christ Jesus and His commandments. These were truly born-again believers. Unlike those today who make this claim, where this has been become a catchphrase used to place themselves above others. We are called to be a witness to all even if we are to face torture or trials unto death. We can see this in the prophecy to some of the seven Churches. This is a message most modern-day preaching lacks. It is not pleasant to have to face this part of the message but many believers in other parts of the world die tortuous deaths daily as witnesses of Jesus' promise of eternal life. We are to love God enough to face anything, for we are not to be afraid of what can destroy the body but that which can destroy the soul.

So now see if you are able to perceive the meaning of the messages to each of the seven churches with new perspective and enhanced understanding of how they apply to us now and for all time. See how they are not fitting into His plans for the Church. See how He is demanding that they turn away from their evil ways. Let's use the looking glass of the Church functioning properly, in kingdom mode, in comparison to the functioning of the seven Churches.

The original participants (those at Pentecost) who had received the fullness of Jesus Christ lived according to a new standard. They lived a kingdom lifestyle which was brought about through a miraculous occurrence on the day of Pentecost. They had been converted to the image of Christ Jesus. They now had the true love of God in their hearts to the point that they loved their neighbors as themselves and loved God with all their heart mind and strength. Love of God and love of their fellow saints was their motivation for all that they did. So, they came to understand that nothing was theirs but it all belonged to God. They gave up ownership of their property and they had all things in common. They no longer needed to live the Old Testament law of tithing. They came to a point where they wanted to give out of love for the brethren. They gave not just because they knew someone which had a need but they gave out of the generosity God had provided them that all might share in the goodness of His bounty on this earth. They worshiped God in spirit and truth so there was no separation in their response to Him. They followed the promptings and work of the Spirit hence there was power resident to do the work that Christ told us when He said greater things will you do than I have done. They gave because they wanted everyone to be treated fairly due to God's love for all His creation and their love for the fellowship. They knew none should be deprived in the kingdom and all should share and share as they had received of His abundance. To them everyone in the Church was his sister and brother and his mother and father. They were all one family. This is not the communist philosophy where they try to accomplish equality thorough force. This is not something we can just teach although the apostles tried. It requires a transformed spirit and commitment to living here on earth as it is in heaven. It requires a new heart and understanding and level of love yet to be experienced in the modern Church. They did not need to be told or forced to study scripture because they had the Holy Spirit as their tutor and they were able to receive and understand the scripture as it was intended to be read and understood. They were driven by a deep desire to study which came as a result of the new heart they had for God. They knew God and walked in unity with Him. Yet there were those who had not reached this level of transformation and some who even tried to fake it. You see we can't fool God nor can we pull the wool over His eyes. Examine the case of Ananias and Saphira. Christ allowed counterfeits to come among them, the thorns in the parable of the sower. Yes, Jesus allowed them all to exist together.

ACTS 5:1-15 AMPLIFIED BIBLE (AMP)
Fate of Ananias and Sapphira

1 Now a man named Ananias, with his wife Sapphira, sold a piece of property,

2 and with his wife's full knowledge [and complicity] he kept back some of the proceeds, bringing only a [a]portion of it, and set it at the apostles' feet.

3 But Peter said, "Ananias, why has Satan filled your heart to lie to the Holy Spirit and [secretly] keep back for yourself some of the proceeds [from the sale] of the land?

4 As long as it remained [unsold], did it not remain your own [to do with as you pleased]? And after it was sold, was the money not under your control? Why is it that you have conceived this act [of hypocrisy and deceit] in your heart? You have not [simply] lied to people, but to God."

5 And hearing these words, Ananias fell down suddenly and died; and great fear and awe gripped those who heard of it.

6 And the young men [in the congregation] got up and wrapped up the body, and carried it out and buried it.

⁷ Now after an interval of about three hours his wife came in, not knowing what had happened.
⁸ Peter asked her, "Tell me whether you sold your land for so much?" And she said, "Yes, for so much."
⁹ Then Peter said to her, "How could you two have agreed together to put the Spirit of the Lord to the test? Look! The feet of those who have buried your husband are at the door, and they will carry you out also."
¹⁰ And at once she fell down at his feet and died; and the young men came in and found her dead, and they carried her out and buried her beside her husband.
¹¹ And great fear and awe gripped the whole Church, and all who heard about these things.
¹² At the hands of the apostles many signs and wonders (attesting miracles) were continually taking place among the people. And by common consent they all met together [at the temple] in [the covered porch called] Solomon's portico.
¹³ But none of the rest [of the people, the non-believers] dared to associate with them; however, the people were holding them in high esteem and were speaking highly of them.
¹⁴ More and more believers in the Lord, crowds of men and women, were constantly being added to their number,
¹⁵ to such an extent that they even carried their sick out into the streets and put them on cots and sleeping pads, so that when Peter came by at least his shadow might fall on one of them [with healing power].

Footnotes:
Acts 5:2 Ananias wanted everyone to think that he had turned over all the money from the sale, so secretly holding some back was essentially embezzling. If he had been honest and told Peter that he had kept some of the money, he would have done nothing wrong.

We don't understand that God can act swiftly. This is why we are provided with the letters to the seven Churches. Jesus is pointing out the thorns in their midst and ours. We as they need to be made aware of them and to rid themselves of them to perform the work they were called to perform and what they were called to be as His true disciples. He demands believers who are truly born from above. He points us to those good and righteous things incorporated in the functioning of His work in the life of the Church. He wants us to learn by example. He wants us to know what lies ahead and what we are facing right now.

As stated in Revelation 1:19, He wants us to know the past, present and future so we can be prepared as a parent tries to teach His children. Look at these from the perspective with which they were intended. Heed the warnings of things which can impede the work of Jesus and heed the message of those things which can enhance His work. Finally understand that we as His Church will face buffeting imprisonment and possibly even suffer death as a result of our commitment to Him. Yes, we are all going to die one day, just look around. These bodies are programmed to die. Death of the body is inevitable. It is a truth we don't like to face so we live as though it will never happen.

Repent if anything in your old life is carried over into your church life which fits under the label of sins. Otherwise Jesus will not allow you to continue and eventually remove you from your role which is to be a light unto the world. Just as Paul told new converts that they were to no longer, steal, cheat, lie, commit sexual immorality, worship anything but the true God or continue any sin which you are committing and be transformed by the renewing of your mind in your spirit by the gift of the Holy Spirit. Again, I share this from the letter to the Ephesians.

>   ***EPHESIANS 4:17-30 AMPLIFIED BIBLE (AMP)***
> ***The Christian's Walk***
> *[17] So this I say, and solemnly affirm together with the Lord [as in His presence], that you must no longer live as the [unbelieving] Gentiles live, in the futility of their minds [and in the foolishness and emptiness of their souls],*
> *[18] for their [moral] understanding is darkened and their reasoning is clouded; [they are] alienated and self-banished from the life of God [with no share in it; this is] because of the [willful] ignorance and spiritual blindness that is [deep-seated] within them, because of the hardness and insensitivity of their heart.*
> *[19] And they, [the ungodly in their spiritual apathy], having become callous and unfeeling, have given themselves over [as prey] to unbridled sensuality, eagerly craving the practice of every kind of impurity [that their desires may demand].*
> *[20] But you did not learn Christ in this way!*
> *[21] If in fact you have [really] heard Him and have been taught by Him, just as truth is in Jesus [revealed in His life and personified in Him],*

²² that, regarding your previous way of life, you put off your old self [completely discard your fromer nature], which is being corrupted through deceitful desires,
²³ and be continually renewed in the spirit of your mind [having a fresh, untarnished mental and spiritual attitude],
²⁴ and put on the new self [the regenerated and renewed nature], created in God's image, [godlike] in the righteousness and holiness of the truth [living in a way that expresses to God your gratitude for your salvation].
²⁵ Therefore, rejecting all falsehood [whether lying, defrauding, telling half-truths, spreading rumors, any such as these], speak truth each one with his neighbor, for we are all parts of one another [and we are all parts of the body of Christ].
²⁶ Be angry [at sin—at immorality, at injustice, at ungodly behavior], yet do not sin; do not let your anger [cause you shame, nor allow it to] last until the sun goes down.
²⁷ And do not give the devil an opportunity [to lead you into sin by holding a grudge, or nurturing anger, or harboring resentment, or cultivating bitterness].
²⁸ The thief [who has become a believer] must no longer steal, but instead he must work hard [making an honest living], producing that which is good with his own hands, so that he will have something to share with those in need.
²⁹ Do not let unwholesome [foul, profane, worthless, vulgar] words ever come out of your mouth, but only such speech as is good for building up others, according to the need and the occasion, so that it will be a blessing to those who hear [you speak].
³⁰ And do not grieve the Holy Spirit of God [but seek to please Him], by whom you were sealed and marked [branded as God's own] for the day of redemption [the final deliverance from the consequences of sin].

Summary

We see here several important truths:
1. Jesus supplies the faithful with a regenerated lifestyle which resembles that of His. This is what is required to be a truly born-again believer.
2. Some of the characteristics which are evidences of being born again were as follows:

a. They loved their brethren enough to give without reservation.
   b. They no longer saw the need to hoard possessions. They were generous.
   c. They met and studied the scripture as a group to gain better understanding. The Holy spirit was the authority for this. They did not have bible scholars teaching them.
   d. Worship was shared by all.
   e. Each Church had those called of God who served as their priesthood.
   f. The elements of the devil crept in as they expanded the membership. This included self-proclaimed ministers and deceitful members whose goal it was to draw them from Christ.
   g. They were provided the gifts of miracles as it met the needs of Christ based on their faith. They cast out devils, healed the sick and performed many other works of the Spirit.
3. His justice requires punishment of those who do not adhere to His standards after they have agreed to His conditions.
4. We are rewarded in eternal life in accordance with our response to Him here on this earth.
5. Eternal life was provided as a result of our commitment to Jesus as our savior.
6. The life of a believer will not always be easy, nor will we always find the fulfilment of His promises here on earth as we would like to see it. There will be times of turmoil and times of testing which are all to go through. This is not the feel-good gospel many preach today.
7. We are all going to face temptation in some form. All of which is for the glory of God because those who have truly been transformed can overcome this through trust in Him. This is the patience we have to have is to trust that eventually justice will be provided.

Now let's go on to the prophesy to the first Church in this group.

CHAPTER 3

Prophecy to the Church of Ephesus

> **REVELATION 2:1-7 KING JAMES VERSION (KJV)**
> *¹ Unto the angel of the Church of Ephesus write; These things saith he that holdeth the seven stars in his right hand, who walketh in the midst of the seven golden candlesticks;*
> *² I know thy works, and thy labour, and thy patience, and how thou canst not bear them which are evil: and thou hast tried them which say they are apostles, and are not, and hast found them liars:*
> *³ And hast borne, and hast patience, and for my name's sake hast laboured, and hast not fainted.*
> *⁴ Nevertheless I have somewhat against thee, because thou hast left thy first love.*
> *⁵ Remember therefore from whence thou art fallen, and repent, and do the first works; or else I will come unto thee quickly, and will remove thy candlestick out of his place, except thou repent.*
> *⁶ But this thou hast, that thou hatest the deeds of the Nicolaitanes, which I also hate.*
> *⁷ He that hath an ear, let him hear what the Spirit saith unto the Churches; To him that overcometh will I give to eat of the tree of life, which is in the midst of the paradise of God.*

Again, it took the work of the Holy Spirit to get me to know this is the same group of believers that was being addressed in the letter to the Ephesians. Here, Jesus is stating trough prophetic utterance what he sees in the Church at Ephesus (or, the Ephesians as they are called in Paul's letter). We can compare the letter which Paul wrote years earlier and how this group's attitudes are now different. Jesus is providing His loving evaluation of each of seven the churches and telling them what they are doing and what they are about to face. He is chastising those whom He loves.

At Ephesus, He notes and commends the good deeds they have done but identifies that those good deeds are not the most important thing for them to do. What matters most is that they have left their first love. That is, they are no longer following what they **<u>first came to believe</u>**. There was a thorn in their side which needed to be removed.

ACTS 11:1-18 KING JAMES VERSION (KJV)

¹ *And the apostles and brethren that were in Judaea heard that the Gentiles had also received the word of God.*

² *And when Peter was come up to Jerusalem, they that were of the circumcision contended with him,*

³ *Saying, Thou wentest in to men uncircumcised, and didst eat with them.*

⁴ *But Peter rehearsed the matter from the beginning, and expounded it by order unto them, saying,*

⁵ *I was in the city of Joppa praying: and in a trance I saw a vision, A certain vessel descend, as it had been a great sheet, let down from heaven by four corners; and it came even to me:*

⁶ *Upon the which when I had fastened mine eyes, I considered, and saw fourfooted beasts of the earth, and wild beasts, and creeping things, and fowls of the air.*

⁷ *And I heard a voice saying unto me, Arise, Peter; slay and eat.*

⁸ *But I said, Not so, Lord: for nothing common or unclean hath at any time entered into my mouth.*

⁹ *But the voice answered me again from heaven, What God hath cleansed, that call not thou common.*

¹⁰ *And this was done three times: and all were drawn up again into heaven.*

¹¹ *And, behold, immediately there were three men already come unto the house where I was, sent from Caesarea unto me.*

¹² *And the Spirit bade me go with them, nothing doubting. Moreover these six brethren accompanied me, and we entered into the man's house:*

¹³ *And he shewed us how he had seen an angel in his house, which stood and said unto him, Send men to Joppa, and call for Simon, whose surname is Peter;*

¹⁴ *Who shall tell thee words, whereby thou and all thy house shall be saved.*

¹⁵ *And as I began to speak, the Holy Ghost fell on them, as on us at the beginning.*

¹⁶ Then remembered I the word of the Lord, how that he said, John indeed baptized with water; but ye shall be baptized with the Holy Ghost.
¹⁷ Forasmuch then as God gave them the like gift as he did unto us, who believed on the Lord Jesus Christ; what was I, that I could withstand God?
¹⁸ When they heard these things, they held their peace, and glorified God, saying, Then hath God also to the Gentiles granted repentance unto life.

We should note that Jesus uses only a portion of the image presented to John at the beginning of this prophecy in chapter one to describe Himself. He then notes He has the seven stars in His right hand. The right hand with the stars is reminding them that they are not the only Church with which He is communicating. Each star is a leader or angel appointed to lead a particular Church. Each of these leaders are in His hand, which symbolizes they are under His authority, and belong to Him and are to represent Him. It is also reminding them He is the key to eternal life, which they needed to keep foremost in their minds. He is also pointing to the fact their power comes from Him, not just their efforts. He is indicating that they are His possession, not any other.

The image of Jesus walking among the candlesticks symbolizes that He is interested in their actions and is not far off somewhere else. He is close enough to know what is going on in the body and what they have been doing and what needs to be praised and what needs correction. Not only this, He is also there to support them. He reminds them of the changes which they have allowed to occur by their response to the Holy Spirit. He points to the fact that there is yet more they need to do. He tells them that there still a need for further repentance from ungodly works. He lets them know it is a matter of extreme importance for them to pay more attention to the work of the Holy Spirit in them, otherwise, they will no longer be allowed to be His representative. They had not arrived at a fully transformed heart of love for God and the brethren. But they had allowed something else to avert their attention from the Holy Spirit. This became the reason for their works. It has been made known to me that what was central to their problem was pride. This is a tool of the devil which can easily appeal to man's desire to be wanted and revered.

In this scripture we see the Holy Ghost had been received and had produced what we are all to experience, the fire and power of Jesus surging in us. That is, a change had occurred in them and they came to know that through the sacrifice of Christ Jesus, they received forgiveness of sin, they accepted God as the source of all creation and that by the power of His Spirit they could be able to be remade in His image, which would produce within them a new heart and a new mind that put God and His righteousness first. This caused them to love God, Jesus, and their brothers and sisters and helped them to be the kingdom of God here on earth. This is the first priority for us all as Christians. It was the need for them to be reborn and to be remade in His image which was most important, not just doing good works. They needed to keep the goal of Him and His plan to rejuvenate them and release them from the bondage of sin at the forefront of each of their activities. Even though they had accepted this at the beginning, they placed this on hold and started doing things for their own glory. Like most of us, when we see the results of our efforts, we become enamored with our own selves and start to overlook the fact it was God who had placed in us the will to do good works after the fashion in which we were originally created. They had started to turn from glorifying God in what they were accomplishing. It is the fact, a temptation which we all face. We all have to realize that everything we do is for His glory and to prove we are the workmanship of His hands. It is joint accomplishment not ours alone.

He also emphasizes that they needed to be willing to receive His guidance and be willing to follow it. We see the statement "those who have ears to hear" abounds throughout all scripture, indicating it was still our choice either to accept or to reject His instruction. They should have understood from this statement the importance of what was being said.

EPHESIANS 4:17-32 AMPLIFIED BIBLE (AMP)
The Christian's Walk

[17] So this I say, and solemnly affirm together with the Lord [as in His presence], that you must no longer live as the [unbelieving] Gentiles live, in the futility of their minds [and in the foolishness and emptiness of their souls],

[18] for their [moral] understanding is darkened and their reasoning is clouded; [they are] alienated and self-banished from the life of God [with no share in it; this is] because of the [willful] ignorance

and spiritual blindness that is [deep-seated] within them, because of the hardness and insensitivity of their heart.

[19] And they, [the ungodly in their spiritual apathy], having become callous and unfeeling, have given themselves over [as prey] to unbridled sensuality, eagerly craving the practice of every kind of impurity [that their desires may demand].

[20] But you did not learn Christ in this way!

[21] If in fact you have [really] heard Him and have been taught by Him, just as truth is in Jesus [revealed in His life and personified in Him],

[22] that, regarding your previous way of life, you put off your old self [completely discard your fromer nature], which is being corrupted through deceitful desires,

[23] and be continually renewed in the spirit of your mind [having a fresh, untarnished mental and spiritual attitude],

[24] and put on the new self [the regenerated and renewed nature], created in God's image, [godlike] in the righteousness and holiness of the truth [living in a way that expresses to God your gratitude for your salvation].

[25] Therefore, rejecting all falsehood [whether lying, defrauding, telling half-truths, spreading rumors, any such as these], speak truth each one with his neighbor, for we are all parts of one another [and we are all parts of the body of Christ].

[26] Be angry [at sin—at immorality, at injustice, at ungodly behavior], yet do not sin; do not let your anger [cause you shame, nor allow it to] last until the sun goes down.

[27] And do not give the devil an opportunity [to lead you into sin by holding a grudge, or nurturing anger, or harboring resentment, or cultivating bitterness].

[28] The thief [who has become a believer] must no longer steal, but instead he must work hard [making an honest living], producing that which is good with his own hands, so that he will have something to share with those in need.

[29] Do not let unwholesome [foul, profane, worthless, vulgar] words ever come out of your mouth, but only such speech as is good for building up others, according to the need and the occasion, so that it will be a blessing to those who hear [you speak].

[30] And do not grieve the Holy Spirit of God [but seek to please Him], by whom you were sealed and marked [branded as God's own] for the day of redemption [the final deliverance from the consequences of sin].

> **³¹** *Let all bitterness and wrath and anger and clamor [perpetual animosity, resentment, strife, fault-finding] and slander be put away from you, along with every kind of malice [all spitefulness, verbal abuse, malevolence].*
> **³²** *Be kind and helpful to one another, tender-hearted [compassionate, understanding], forgiving one another [readily and freely], just as God in Christ also forgave [a]you.*
>
> Footnotes:
> Ephesians 4:32 Two early mss read us.

The center of all activity which we take part in, is our loving God with all our heart mind and strength and loving our neighbors as ourselves. This how we become one with Him and each other. Without this level of love, everything we do is worthless and does not matter. Love is the basis of all Christian activity whether it is for someone else or ourselves. It takes love to truly forgive and forget. It takes love to accept everyone as a brother or sister or as a mother or father. It takes love to minister to the need of someone you don't know or have never seen. It takes love to understand that all that has been provided on earth is for the benefit of all and there should be a proper balance in distributing the wealth God has provided. It takes love to forgive others. Love is needed to accept all that we have to face to honor our commitment to Christ and to others. It is love that gives not because someone deserves it, but because it is a gift from God to share liberally just as it has been provided for us. By His power we can achieve the elements of true love which is the same as His and become one with Him and each other.

It takes Godly love to accept that we are all created equal in Christ Jesus. It takes Godly love to trust that no matter what comes our way, we can handle it for the love of our God. It takes Godly love to trust in the fairness of God and accept that Jesus is all we need to be like Him. It takes Godly love to want to be like God and Jesus and to be willing to allow the Holy Spirit to root out all our sinful ways and replace them with the righteous love of God. It takes love to evaluate when others do wrong the need to have that pointed out. It takes Godly love to hate sin and how it can destroy the destiny of an individual. It takes Godly love to have the patience to endure the troubles on this earth, trusting that God will deliver us in the end. It takes Godly love to wait on the resurrection of our bodies so we can enjoy being in His presence for eternity.

Jesus points out that both He and these Christians hate the deeds of the Nicolaitans. Throughout my studies no one seems to have an understanding or seems to have found out what it was the Nicolaitans did. Jesus wants us to understand that there are religious practices which are revolting to Him and that we are to judge these just as He does. Yes, we are to judge wrong doing.

Not too long ago in a dream the Lord began to show to me what the practice of the Nicolaitans was. He showed me a three-sided chute. This chute was similar to a box with one open end and no top. It only had three sides. It had a shape such that the closed end was the highest point. The two sides each side sloped downward from the closed end toward the open end. Then there were items which were being placed in it. At first, I could not focus enough to comprehend what these were. It was a blur. At the end of this experience I was told that what was being placed in this chute were babies, which were being offered up as a sacrifice to some made up god.

I know from my studies of the Latin language in high school and from other historic books which I have read in my lifetime that it was not uncommon for people to offer up children as sacrifices. I can recall that it was a common practice to take unwanted children and place them in the woods for them to die or to be killed by wild animals.

Even in our day and time, in China they limited families to no more than two children and that they also practiced taking unwanted children (those who exceeded the government mandate) and placing them out in the wild to die. They were also known to mutilate women to prevent them from having children. China had set a limit of one child per family and which has now increased this to two. I understand they may consider with doing away with this practice altogether since many are aborting female children in favor of males. I understand they are receiving increasing protest from countries around the world about this policy. We see worldwide where children are being aborted for the sake of finances, shame, pleasure and other humanistic desires and reasoning. It is a practice which God hates among many others, but He especially hates the shedding of innocent blood. He sees human life as a divine given right which He and only He has the right to determine when it begins and when it ends.

Summary

Let's summarize what there is about Ephesus which is of lasting value. We can see that the letter Paul wrote to them had a profound effect, as they had responded to it and responded to the work of the Holy Spirit. They had let pride in what they did overshadow the purpose behind what they were doing. They had missed what was most important, their spiritual transformation.

1. There had been a move of the Holy Spirit which led them to start doing good works.
2. They had needed to reached a new level of love for God and each other but were somehow lost insight into this.
3. They had gained the knowledge of that which is evil in the sight of God and they did not tolerate it among them.
4. They had gained enough knowledge to be able to spot false doctrine and those who promoted it. This came through studying scripture under the tutelage of the Holy Spirit, they were able to identify what was false teaching just as Jesus did when confronted by the twisted interpretation of scripture by the devil at the end of His forty day fast.

> **MATTHEW 7:10-16 KING JAMES VERSION (KJV)**
> [10] *Or if he ask a fish, will he give him a serpent?*
> [11] *If ye then, being evil, know how to give good gifts unto your children, how much more shall your Father which is in heaven give good things to them that ask him?*
> [12] *Therefore all things whatsoever ye would that men should do to you, do ye even so to them: for this is the law and the prophets.*
> [13] *Enter ye in at the strait gate: for wide is the gate, and broad is the way, that leadeth to destruction, and many there be which go in thereat:*
> [14] *Because strait is the gate, and narrow is the way, which leadeth unto life, and few there be that find it.*
> [15] *Beware of false prophets, which come to you in sheep's clothing, but inwardly they are ravening wolves.*
> [16] *Ye shall know them by their fruits. Do men gather grapes of thorns, or figs of thistles?*

5. They understood doctrines which were evil and learned to hate them as Jesus did. They were converted to the point they had

an understanding of religious practices which are born of evil (the devil).

> **2 TIMOTHY 4:2-4 KING JAMES VERSION (KJV)**
> *² Preach the word; be instant in season, out of season; reprove, rebuke, exhort with all long suffering and doctrine.*
> *³ For the time will come when they will not endure sound doctrine; but after their own lusts shall they heap to themselves teachers, having itching ears;*
> *⁴ And they shall turn away their ears from the truth, and shall be turned unto fables.*

6. They were operating in light of their need to wait upon the Lord and the need to be willing to persevere as long as they needed to.
7. They had stopped doing what was their first love; which was to be reborn and to spread the work of the cross, the crucifixion and the offer of eternal life to those who were willing to repent.

These are the eternal truths which we are to gain from this book.

1. Do good works designed by God. Scripture contains these in many forms and actions. Paul outlines most of these in His letter to the Ephesians years prior to the presentation of this prophecy. The beginning and ending of our good works should be to glorify God and Christ Jesus.
2. All that we do should be driven by our love for God and our fellowman.
3. Hate evil and those who promote it. Scripture provides instances which guide us into understanding how these are implemented. Prayerfully read these as presented in the letter to the Ephesians by Paul.
4. Study the scripture and allow the Holy Spirit to teach you to be knowledgeable of what God hates and loves so that we can be able to identify these.
5. Study the scripture and allow the Holy Spirit to teach you the difference between false doctrine and correct doctrine and how to spot phonies claiming to be of Christ.
6. Be fervent in proclaiming the gospel of Christ and His call to repentance and the offer of the gift of eternal life.
7. If we are willing, He will bring us understanding. Those Churches which have ears to hear let them hear. Note the expression here in Revelation 2:7 clearly designates that it is a

message to every Church then and now and in the future. What is being said is for every Church to learn.

> **REVELATION 2:7 KING JAMES VERSION (KJV)**
> *⁷ He that hath an ear, let him hear what the Spirit saith unto the Churches; To him that overcometh will I give to eat of the tree of life, which is in the midst of the paradise of God.*

8. They were being called to establish the highest level of response to His work in them.
9. Seek and first the kingdom which is the love of God and our brothers and sisters. Be fervent in proclaiming this by your lifestyle and through your actions in order that others might be freed from the bondage of sin and join us in eternity.
10. Walk in the light of the Spirit to be able to repent from dead works and be converted to the righteous works.
11. Heed the admonition of the ministers **_who are called_** to lead the Churches in the right path. Ministers are called to minister in righteousness. **_Prove the false ministers as liars._**
12. Be alert to the instruction of Christ provided through the gift of prophecy.
13. **_Beware of those who claim to be prophets but who are not called of God._**
14. **_Don't let pride overcome you._**

CHAPTER 4

Prophecy to the Church in Smyrna

REVELATION 2:8-11 KING JAMES VERSION (KJV)
8 And unto the angel of the Church in Smyrna write; These things saith the first and the last, which was dead, and is alive;
9 I know thy works, and tribulation, and poverty, (but thou art rich) and I know the blasphemy of them which say they are Jews, and are not, but are the synagogue of Satan.
10 Fear none of those things which thou shalt suffer: behold, the devil shall cast some of you into prison, that ye may be tried; and ye shall have tribulation ten days: be thou faithful unto death, and I will give thee a crown of life.
11 He that hath an ear, let him hear what the Spirit saith unto the Churches; He that overcometh shall not be hurt of the second death.

To Smyrna He provides something different. He starts by reassuring them that He was the true Christ and they could be confident that He was alive eternal. Eternal life is the essence of what He provides. It is the nature of His being. Without him there is no existence. This emphasizes that they too have eternal life because they have the same spirit which raised Jesus from the grave. As is promised in scripture, this same spirit will raise us into eternal life as well.

1 CORINTHIANS 10:2-4 KING JAMES VERSION (KJV)
2 And were all baptized unto Moses in the cloud and in the sea;
3 And did all eat the same spiritual meat;

> ⁴ *And did all drink the same spiritual drink: for they drank of that spiritual Rock that followed them: and that Rock was Christ.*
> **2 CORINTHIANS 3:17-18 KING JAMES VERSION (KJV)**
> ¹⁷ *Now the Lord is that Spirit: and where the Spirit of the Lord is, there is liberty.*
> ¹⁸ *But we all, with open face beholding as in a glass the glory of the Lord, are changed into the same image from glory to glory, even as by the Spirit of the Lord.*
> **2 CORINTHIANS 4:12-14 KING JAMES VERSION (KJV)**
> ¹² *So then death worketh in us, but life in you.*
> ¹³ *We having the same spirit of faith, according as it is written, I believed, and therefore have I spoken; we also believe, and therefore speak;*
> ¹⁴ *Knowing that he which raised up the Lord Jesus shall raise up us also by Jesus, and shall present us with you.*

You see, Jesus begins pointing out that they were doing the right things; the good things which the Holy Spirit had implanted in them. He makes this known by a simple statement. Jesus is indicating that He is pleased in their efforts. He provides in a few words so much more than we can see. What He knows is so important. The fact that He knows their works expresses that He has been observing them and is aware of their spiritual condition. Jesus sees all things as spiritual. He is expressing He finds no fault in their motives or their attitudes. He expresses in these few words that He accepts they have complied with His will and they should keep doing the things they are doing. In modern day vernacular they were in the groove. You see they were living a kingdom lifestyle. They had received the fullness of His conversion and their lives reflected His image here on earth (the kingdom of God).

Now here is the kicker. He tells them the source of their agitation was coming from those who were not true worshipers but those who were followers of the devil. Here, Jesus identifies that their struggle was a result of the spiritual wickedness in high places not just flesh and blood. We have to come to understand the degree of influence which the devil has in the life of man. Again, it is the choice we all have to make which is to either follow our conscience or denounce our conscience, that God has programmed. When we denounce our conscience, we open the door for the control by the devil. The result is that we become a puppet of the devil to inflict pain and suffering.

Jesus then begins to warn them of the tribulation which they were about to face because of their allegiance to Him. He tells them they can expect to suffer at the hands of the so-called Jewish community, even unto death. Jesus tells them to not fear this because of Him they would not have to suffer the second death. Jesus is reinforcing the fact that they have eternal life. It is a second reinforcement of His promise that He has overcome death and the grave. The second death is the punishment of the devil and His followers.

He even provides a time period for the length of their suffering. Now the 10 days which He states is not defined as the standard 24-hour day as we know it to be. Many bible scholars interpret that whenever days are stated as prophecy that the standard to be used is one day is equal to one thousand years to the Lord. I am not led to use this as a standard. The direction I have received is that for the next 10 years they would experience this turmoil. Jesus provided them a definite period of time because wanted them to understand that this would not be an indefinite state. Jesus did not them to be discouraged by the length of time they were to face these trials and tribulations. This is because some had yet to reach the point of full conversion to where time on this earth did not matter. We can compare this to those who were willing to be eaten by lions, or burned at the stake or have suffered all manner of horrible mistreatment. A fate most of us modern western Christians don't even consider as a possibility. That is why we so readily accept the doctrine of the rapture. Here Jesus is relating that suffering on this earth will continue with us involved. He does not remove us from these horrible circumstances, but He stands there with us and supports us every step of the way. It brings to life the words in the 23rd Psalm "Yeah though I walk through the valley of the shadow of death I will fear no evil for you are with me". They were in the shadow of death and Jesus was giving them the understanding this was not just the world they were facing and to be strong and confident.

PSALM 23:1-6 KING JAMES VERSION (KJV)
^{1} The Lord is my shepherd; I shall not want.
^{2} He maketh me to lie down in green pastures: he leadeth me beside the still waters.
^{3} He restoreth my soul: he leadeth me in the paths of righteousness for his name's sake.

> [4] *Yea, though I walk through the valley of the shadow of death, I will fear no evil: for thou art with me; thy rod and thy staff they comfort me.*
> [5] *Thou preparest a table before me in the presence of mine enemies: thou anointest my head with oil; my cup runneth over.*
> [6] *Surely goodness and mercy shall follow me all the days of my life: and I will dwell in the house of the Lord for ever.*

We often complain about the smallest discomforts but these men, women and children were about to face the ultimate of pain challenges; that of torture and acts meant to disgrace them and their beliefs just as Jesus suffered when He went to the cross. Jesus warned this is an inevitable part of discipleship. We are to be willing and aware that this can and will happen to those who are His true disciples. This is a warning we all must accept and come to realize. The walk of discipleship will not be easy for all. It requires the strength that only comes through Him. That is why we are called to be a peculiar people not like everyone else but distinguished by our Love for God and love for our fellow brothers and sisters.

MATTHEW 10:37-39 KING JAMES VERSION (KJV)

> [37] *He that loveth father or mother more than me is not worthy of me: and he that loveth son or daughter more than me is not worthy of me.*
> [38] *And he that taketh not his cross, and followeth after me, is not worthy of me.*
> [39] *He that findeth his life shall lose it: and he that loseth his life for my sake shall find it.*

LUKE 14:26-28 AMPLIFIED BIBLE (AMP)

> [26] *"If anyone comes to Me, and does not [a]hate his own father and mother and wife and children and brothers and sisters, yes, and even his own life [in the sense of indifference to or relative disregard for them in comparison with his attitude toward God]—he cannot be My disciple.*
> [27] *Whoever does not carry his own cross [expressing a willingness to endure whatever may come] and follow after Me [believing in Me, conforming to My example in living and, if need be, suffering or perhaps dying because of faith in Me] cannot be My disciple.*
> [28] *For which one of you, when he wants to build a watchtower [for his guards], does not first sit down and calculate the cost, to see if he has enough to finish it?*
>
> **Footnotes:**

> *Luke 14:26 An exaggerated figure of speech indicating a lesser degree of love, not actual hostility or aversion toward one's earthly family.*

Now from this I have a hard time seeing or accepting the doctrine of the rapture. You can see from this scripture that Jesus does not remove the testimony of His saints from danger or remove them from the tribulations which they were to face. Here Jesus reassures their willingness to endure the tribulations to be a testimony to those who might be able to be saved from the grip of the devil. He also uses the tenacity and diligence of His saints as a witness to the wickedness which was predominant in this society so that the justice of God will be enforced at the last day. We are a testimony that God was right in having chosen the way of the cross as the correct decision for providing salvation to mankind.

He mentions that they are poor and don't have a lot but this is not something which should cause them to worry. Release from poverty on earth is not promised in the doctrine of Jesus. The release He promises is the release from the grasp of sin. Many modern-day Christians have been deluded in believing we deserve riches here on this earth. Jesus even taught that the rich should divest themselves of riches and distribute it to the poor which is what the Pentecost converts did. He points out those in Smyrna were not rich in worldly terms. He states, but "they are rich". What does He mean by this? Scripture tells us to accumulate treasures in heaven, not on this earth. It is the work of the Spirit in us which brings the benefits and riches of God for us all to share. These are both physical and spiritual. Though we might not see them as physical, the spiritual is the one which is of everlasting importance. To God all things are spiritual because He is the source of all living.

> **MATTHEW 6:1-25 KING JAMES VERSION (KJV)**
> *[1] Take heed that ye do not your alms before men, to be seen of them: otherwise ye have no reward of your Father which is in heaven.*
> *[2] Therefore when thou doest thine alms, do not sound a trumpet before thee, as the hypocrites do in the synagogues and in the streets, that they may have glory of men. Verily I say unto you, They have their reward.*
> *[3] But when thou doest alms, let not thy left hand know what thy right hand doeth:*

⁴ That thine alms may be in secret: and thy Father which seeth in secret himself shall reward thee openly.

⁵ And when thou prayest, thou shalt not be as the hypocrites are: for they love to pray standing in the synagogues and in the corners of the streets, that they may be seen of men. Verily I say unto you, They have their reward.

⁶ But thou, when thou prayest, enter into thy closet, and when thou hast shut thy door, pray to thy Father which is in secret; and thy Father which seeth in secret shall reward thee openly.

⁷ But when ye pray, use not vain repetitions, as the heathen do: for they think that they shall be heard for their much speaking.

⁸ Be not ye therefore like unto them: for your Father knoweth what things ye have need of, before ye ask him.

⁹ After this manner therefore pray ye: Our Father which art in heaven, Hallowed be thy name.

¹⁰ Thy kingdom come, Thy will be done in earth, as it is in heaven.

¹¹ Give us this day our daily bread.

¹² And forgive us our debts, as we forgive our debtors.

¹³ And lead us not into temptation, but deliver us from evil: For thine is the kingdom, and the power, and the glory, for ever. Amen.

¹⁴ For if ye forgive men their trespasses, your heavenly Father will also forgive you:

¹⁵ But if ye forgive not men their trespasses, neither will your Father forgive your trespasses.

¹⁶ Moreover when ye fast, be not, as the hypocrites, of a sad countenance: for they disfigure their faces, that they may appear unto men to fast. Verily I say unto you, They have their reward.

¹⁷ But thou, when thou fastest, anoint thine head, and wash thy face;

¹⁸ That thou appear not unto men to fast, but unto thy Father which is in secret: and thy Father, which seeth in secret, shall reward thee openly.

¹⁹ Lay not up for yourselves treasures upon earth, where moth and rust doth corrupt, and where thieves break through and steal:

²⁰ But lay up for yourselves treasures in heaven, where neither moth nor rust doth corrupt, and where thieves do not break through nor steal:

²¹ For where your treasure is, there will your heart be also.

²² The light of the body is the eye: if therefore thine eye be single, thy whole body shall be full of light.

²³ But if thine eye be evil, thy whole body shall be full of darkness. If therefore the light that is in thee be darkness, how great is that darkness!
²⁴ No man can serve two masters: for either he will hate the one, and love the other; or else he will hold to the one, and despise the other. Ye cannot serve God and mammon.
²⁵ Therefore I say unto you, Take no thought for your life, what ye shall eat, or what ye shall drink; nor yet for your body, what ye shall put on. Is not the life more than meat, and the body than raiment?

Jesus was pointing to the fact that there was a rich reservoir of things which they had accumulated which are not of this world. Our humanness causes us to want to seek comfort and well-being here on this earth. Scripture points to the fact that we are not to accumulate riches on this earth for the sake of this life because all these things are not eternal and do not provide the true riches which we are to accumulate. He is providing a message that most of us would rather not accept because of our selfish desires. It is the opposite of the prosperity gospel which is preached in today's pulpits. We are constantly being bombarded with messages that God wants us to be rich but it this is not what the scripture as a whole dictate. Yes, God wants us to share in His riches but it is not in the way many are presenting today. Many preachers today teach the goal of ministry is to live in the lap of luxury and to possess as much as they can. This was the same trap the ministers at the time of Christ on this earth had fallen into. If Christ felt it was necessary to be rich on this earth then we would automatically become rich when we accept Christ as our savior. Those who do gain riches do not understand the reason for them to have riches is to be able to meet the needs of the poor and needy. They are not to be wasted on themselves and their own selfish pleasures. We are called to share and share alike in the riches which He has provided that we all may benefit from them, not just a few. Jesus was recognizing this principle in this statement. He states He makes the rain to fall on the good, bad and ugly because He loves His creation. None of us can survive without water. Water is necessary for our bodies to survive. Even in the desert we find plants which are called by some resurrection plants because they only show life when water is present.

I fell into the trap that those in this country and most worldwide have accepted. That is, we should use as much of our income as we can for our worldly comfort and only share a small token with others. We designate that small token as our duty to pay tithes. Our greed why most of us in the USA live paycheck to paycheck. This so we can accumulate as much of the worldly goods as we can for our comfort and convenience. Now I am locked into a situation where I don't have much excess to share with my brothers and sisters in Christ as I should. I am not advocating that we should choose to live a life of poverty as some do, but we should be considering that Jesus wants all to share as needed in the goodness He has provided. In other words, those in His kingdom should not lack for anything they need. One sign or identifier that the kingdom is here on earth will be when we are converted into Christ's image and there will be no poor among us. I don't advise promoting statement that we will always have the poor among us. This message was provided to those who have not yet been converted into Jesus' image and do not love as Jesus does. Jesus made this statement to the unbelieving. He was identifying that as long as they remained in their sinful state this is the accepted standard. As long as we decide that we are unwilling to love as Jesus loves, yes, there will be poor among us. In His kingdom it is not to be so.

JEREMIAH 10:12-14 KING JAMES VERSION (KJV)

[12] He hath made the earth by his power, he hath established the world by his wisdom, and hath stretched out the heavens by his discretion.

[13] When he uttereth his voice, there is a multitude of waters in the heavens, and he causeth the vapours to ascend from the ends of the earth; he maketh lightnings with rain, and bringeth forth the wind out of his treasures.

[14] Every man is brutish in his knowledge: every founder is confounded by the graven image: for his molten image is falsehood, and there is no breath in them.

JEREMIAH 10:12-14 AMPLIFIED BIBLE (AMP)

[12] God made the earth by His power; He established the world by His wisdom And by His understanding and skill He has stretched out the heavens.

[13] When He utters His voice, there is a tumult of [a]waters in the heavens, And He causes the clouds and the mist to ascend from the end of the earth; He makes lightning for the rain,

And brings out the wind from His treasuries and from His storehouses.

PROPHECY TO THE SEVEN CHURCHES: PART 1 • 49

> [14] *Every man has become [like a brute] irrational and stupid, without knowledge [of God]; Every goldsmith is shamed by his carved idols; For his molten images are frauds and lies, And there is no breath in them.*
>
> Footnotes:
> *Jeremiah 10:13 Some ancient people believed that the sky was a canopy over the earth and that God stored rainwater behind it. Therefore, it rained only when God opened the windows of heaven.*

His intent is that we all are to share in the things He provides. Therefore, in heavenly terms of the spiritual, their wealth was such that no one could take it away. He has more in store for us in heaven than we can ever accumulate here on earth. They had received the gift of forgiveness of sin and eternal life and the Holy Spirit complete with the gifts of power which He brings with Him. Their hope as is ours was that in the future they would abide with God in His heavenly palace, in His house. Jesus sees their financial matters and it was of concern to Him. Jesus is aware of each part of our lives.

He lets us know we are not alone in our suffering and that He is standing right there with us. He was assuring them that they had power in the Holy Spirit to withstand all they were about to face. Jesus understands that the perfect love which they had would prevent them from fearing anything which they were going to have to face.

Jesus let them know they would face many tribulations both mental and physical and not to be concerned about this. This tribulation was not of His making but He was there with them and with Him they would endure to the end. You see true worshipers will receive the criticism of the religious community because they go against the grain and are not in it for wealth or fame or glory for themselves but to express the righteousness of God here on this earth. It is God's loving righteousness which requires Him to allow these things to occur so that He has an airtight case for the crimes being committed. We plead to be protected from the enemy but God is our protection and in spite of the fact He has to allow evil to exist. We don't understand that He is by our side even to the death of our mortal bodies. It is His will that we are to follow Him even when the situation calls for us to suffer either physically and mentally. Spiritually, we can always have peace in Him through the power of His spirit. Yes, they were told to be patient unto death and to trust God to make recompense for this at the appointed time based on His wisdom. Herein is the embodiment of the truth of forgiveness. We must trust in Him and His integrity to properly repay evil with true justice. This is not the good news many of us want to hear but that's the way it is. God has to allow sin to go to its final result because the deed has to be completed for evidence to punish people. It is not that He wants this to occur this way but His justice requires it. His justice also requires us to accept that He will repay us and comfort us for the suffering here on this earth. We have to remember we were also, at one time, the source of someone else's suffering.

Wow! This is a message we have a hard time accepting and understanding. We see the word "patience" used in the context of the messages to these churches quite a bit. This is the patience which we must have. We are to trust God to make all things right. It, for a lot of us will not be here on this earth, but in heaven. It's a hard pill for us to swallow but that is the life we live and something we need to be willing to accept. The wheat and the tares will grow together until the time of the harvest is at hand. The good and bad will exist together.

I must confess I have not understood this message myself until now. In the end everything will be alright and God will make the crooked things straight. I have not delighted in the things I have suffered in this life. Some I have caused because of choices I've made; others are the result of the sin of others, but all in all it is a result of the two forces at work in this world. These forces of that of God, the good, and work of the devil, the evil. We must come to understand this. That is why we were provided this prophesy.

Summary

This is one of the shortest of the evaluations of the seven Churches. In it, Jesus points to His pleasure in that they were doing the good works which God created them for and they demonstrated that they had allowed the rejuvenating work of the Holy Spirit in them. He let them know that even though they were not rich in worldly possessions, which is the human standard, they were rich. They were told just as we are, to not gather treasure here on earth. The Christians at Smyrna had obeyed. They had gained a much greater inheritance, their treasure in heaven. The greatest treasure of all is eternal life and having your name written in the book of life.

He told them about the trials which they were about to experience and to be prepared for the evil which Satan was about to inflict on them. Jesus wanted them to know what Satan was planning to place before them because He knew that were prepared. He told them the source of the coming problems and the resulting outcome. He also provided them a timeline to let them know it would not last forever.

Jesus wants us to understand that it's not His goal for us to be rich in worldly goods but for us to attain the greatest treasure of all, that which is eternal in nature. We are not to put our trust nor are we to desire those things which will fade away and have no eternal value. We know we can't take it with us so we try to get all we can before we leave here. The pharaohs tried to take it with them. Their tombs demonstrate that it will all be left behind for the thief or explorer, but they don't have it with them. The riches which they had buried with them remain. Their caskets and dead bodies remain, so we have the evidence before us, they don't. The only things we can carry with us is the life we have lived. For the true believer, it is the love of God implanted in us and the forgiveness of sin by the sacrifice of Christ Jesus. In the end all things will be set straight by God.

This was a group of mature Christians. They had received, just as the Saints at Pentecost, a transformed spirit modeled after Jesus. Jesus was able to tell them things which baby Christians could not understand. They strength came as result of the power of Godly love, was embedded in them. To them the words Jesus spoke were not words of doom, but glory and honor. Just as Jesus, they accepted this even though it would be painful. They understood they had all of the power of the Godhead with them and they knew even death could not defeat the ultimate purpose of Jesus, which is to provide us eternal life and forgiveness of sin. They knew that their garments had been washed by the blood of the lamb and they could stand before God in confidence knowing they would hear the words, "Well done my good and faithful servants". They knew that Jesus through the Holy Spirit would fulfill the words which Paul stated in Philippians 4:13 "I can do all things through Christ which strengtheneth me.".

So, the eternal truths here are:

1. Here was a group doing everything right yet they were set to face some horrible trials.
2. Being true to the work of Jesus will not necessarily result in a comfortable existence here on this earth.
3. Jesus applauds our good works.
4. The good works we do will not necessarily produce a like response from others.
5. We should not expect to be made rich in this life.
6. The riches which we are to hold on to and develop are the riches which are retained in heaven. These are:
    a. Accepting Jesus as our savior.
    b. Recognizing that God is creator and sustainer of us all.
    c. The knowledge that God is pleased when we do His works on earth.
    d. Love for God and love for our fellow saints.
    e. The knowledge we have eternal life.
7. We are here for the glory of God. Our sickness and our tribulations and trials are all for His glory and for the benefit of all His creation. It is not the sickness or tribulation which glorifies Him but the fact He will eventually bring the correct cure for these. There is a scripture I am led to add here. It is one I have not understood for a long time but now its true meaning is exemplified by their situation.
8. Don't overlook the fact that they could still feel pain and they still had the choice to either hate or love those who inflicted pain and suffering on them.

JOHN 9:1-38 KING JAMES VERSION (KJV)
¹ And as Jesus passed by, he saw a man which was blind from his birth.
² And his disciples asked him, saying, Master, who did sin, this man, or his parents, that he was born blind?
³ Jesus answered, Neither hath this man sinned, nor his parents: but that the works of God should be made manifest in him.
⁴ I must work the works of him that sent me, while it is day: the night cometh, when no man can work.
⁵ As long as I am in the world, I am the light of the world.
⁶ When he had thus spoken, he spat on the ground, and made clay of the spittle, and he anointed the eyes of the blind man with the clay,

⁷ And said unto him, Go, wash in the pool of Siloam, (which is by interpretation, Sent.) He went his way therefore, and washed, and came seeing.
⁸ The neighbours therefore, and they which before had seen him that he was blind, said, Is not this he that sat and begged?
⁹ Some said, This is he: others said, He is like him: but he said, I am he.
¹⁰ Therefore said they unto him, How were thine eyes opened?
¹¹ He answered and said, A man that is called Jesus made clay, and anointed mine eyes, and said unto me, Go to the pool of Siloam, and wash: and I went and washed, and I received sight.
¹² Then said they unto him, Where is he? He said, I know not.
¹³ They brought to the Pharisees him that aforetime was blind.
¹⁴ And it was the sabbath day when Jesus made the clay, and opened his eyes.
¹⁵ Then again the Pharisees also asked him how he had received his sight. He said unto them, He put clay upon mine eyes, and I washed, and do see.
¹⁶ Therefore said some of the Pharisees, This man is not of God, because he keepeth not the sabbath day. Others said, How can a man that is a sinner do such miracles? And there was a division among them.
¹⁷ They say unto the blind man again, What sayest thou of him, that he hath opened thine eyes? He said, He is a prophet.
¹⁸ But the Jews did not believe concerning him, that he had been blind, and received his sight, until they called the parents of him that had received his sight.
¹⁹ And they asked them, saying, Is this your son, who ye say was born blind? how then doth he now see?
²⁰ His parents answered them and said, We know that this is our son, and that he was born blind:
²¹ But by what means he now seeth, we know not; or who hath opened his eyes, we know not: he is of age; ask him: he shall speak for himself.
²² These words spake his parents, because they feared the Jews: for the Jews had agreed already, that if any man did confess that he was Christ, he should be put out of the synagogue.
²³ Therefore said his parents, He is of age; ask him.
²⁴ Then again called they the man that was blind, and said unto him, Give God the praise: we know that this man is a sinner.
²⁵ He answered and said, Whether he be a sinner or no, I know not: one thing I know, that, whereas I was blind, now I see.

> ²⁶ Then said they to him again, What did he to thee? how opened he thine eyes?
> ²⁷ He answered them, I have told you already, and ye did not hear: wherefore would ye hear it again? will ye also be his disciples?
> ²⁸ Then they reviled him, and said, Thou art his disciple; but we are Moses' disciples.
> ²⁹ We know that God spake unto Moses: as for this fellow, we know not from whence he is.
> ³⁰ The man answered and said unto them, Why herein is a marvellous thing, that ye know not from whence he is, and yet he hath opened mine eyes.
> ³¹ Now we know that God heareth not sinners: but if any man be a worshipper of God, and doeth his will, him he heareth.
> ³² Since the world began was it not heard that any man opened the eyes of one that was born blind.
> ³³ If this man were not of God, he could do nothing.
> ³⁴ They answered and said unto him, Thou wast altogether born in sins, and dost thou teach us? And they cast him out.
> ³⁵ Jesus heard that they had cast him out; and when he had found him, he said unto him, Dost thou believe on the Son of God?
> ³⁶ He answered and said, Who is he, Lord, that I might believe on him?
> ³⁷ And Jesus said unto him, Thou hast both seen him, and it is he that talketh with thee.
> ³⁸ And he said, Lord, I believe. And he worshipped him.

9. We will all know in the future the depth of His love.
10. We are to be patient and understand that the promises of God will be fulfilled, maybe not on this earth, but definitely in heaven.
11. We are to endure all things for the glory of God and in the end, He will prove His works are righteous.

> **1 CHRONICLES 16:33-35 KING JAMES VERSION (KJV)**
> ³³ Then shall the trees of the wood sing out at the presence of the Lord, because he cometh to judge the earth.
> ³⁴ O give thanks unto the Lord; for he is good; for his mercy endureth for ever.
> ³⁵ And say ye, Save us, O God of our salvation, and gather us together, and deliver us from the heathen, that we may give thanks to thy holy name, and glory in thy praise.

11. We can expect trouble even unto death as a representative of Christ and we can expect to be a target of resentment from those who are not true Christians. In all of this Christ stands with us.
12. When we demonstrate that we truly have been converted into having the love of God within us we will be able to endure trials and tribulation for His sake and others. Then we will be the true light unto the world.

CHAPTER 5

Prophecy to the Church in Pergamos

> **REVELATION 2:12-17 KING JAMES VERSION (KJV)**
> *¹² And to the angel of the Church in Pergamos write; These things saith he which hath the sharp sword with two edges;*
> *¹³ I know thy works, and where thou dwellest, even where Satan's seat is: and thou holdest fast my name, and hast not denied my faith, even in those days wherein Antipas was my faithful martyr, who was slain among you, where Satan dwelleth.*
> *¹⁴ But I have a few things against thee, because thou hast there them that hold the doctrine of Balaam, who taught Balac to cast a stumblingblock before the children of Israel, to eat things sacrificed unto idols, and to commit fornication.*
> *¹⁵ So hast thou also them that hold the doctrine of the Nicolaitanes, which thing I hate.*
> *¹⁶ Repent; or else I will come unto thee quickly, and will fight against them with the sword of my mouth.*
> *¹⁷ He that hath an ear, let him hear what the Spirit saith unto the Churches; To him that overcometh will I give to eat of the hidden manna, and will give him a white stone, and in the stone a new name written, which no man knoweth saving he that receiveth it.*

Here we see that some of those in Pergamos were holding on to false doctrine and pagan practices even though they said that they had accepted Christ, His gift of forgiveness, the gift of eternal life and the work of the Holy spirit in them. Some were still performing the same things which they had been doing in the past. They were still living as an unbeliever or a pagan life. They were continuing to worship idols and practicing those things which were a part of that religious belief system and had not repented of these things. They were demonstrating that they liked and wanted to continue holding onto their past lives. As Jesus stated about two masters, you will either love one and cling onto him and hate the other, but you can't please both. You eventually will have to choose between the two. That is, you will find conflicts which you cannot resolve. Our tendency toward self-centeredness is what makes this so difficult.

> ***ACTS 15:15-33 KING JAMES VERSION (KJV)***
> *15 And to this agree the words of the prophets; as it is written,*
> *16 After this I will return, and will build again the tabernacle of David, which is fallen down; and I will build again the ruins thereof, and I will set it up:*
> *17 That the residue of men might seek after the Lord, and all the Gentiles, upon whom my name is called, saith the Lord, who doeth all these things.*
> *18 Known unto God are all his works from the beginning of the world.*
> *19 Wherefore my sentence is, that we trouble not them, which from among the Gentiles are turned to God:*
> *20 But that we write unto them, that they abstain from pollutions of idols, and from fornication, and from things strangled, and from blood.*
> *21 For Moses of old time hath in every city them that preach him, being read in the synagogues every sabbath day.*
> *22 Then pleased it the apostles and elders with the whole Church, to send chosen men of their own company to Antioch with Paul and Barnabas; namely, Judas surnamed Barsabas and Silas, chief men among the brethren:*
> *23 And they wrote letters by them after this manner; The apostles and elders and brethren send greeting unto the brethren which are of the Gentiles in Antioch and Syria and Cilicia.*
> *24 Forasmuch as we have heard, that certain which went out from us have troubled you with words, subverting your souls, saying, Ye must be circumcised, and keep the law: to whom we gave no such commandment:*
> *25 It seemed good unto us, being assembled with one accord, to send chosen men unto you with our beloved Barnabas and Paul,*
> *26 Men that have hazarded their lives for the name of our Lord Jesus Christ.*

²⁷ *We have sent therefore Judas and Silas, who shall also tell you the same things by mouth.*
²⁸ *For it seemed good to the Holy Ghost, and to us, to lay upon you no greater burden than these necessary things;*
²⁹ *That ye abstain from meats offered to idols, and from blood, and from things strangled, and from fornication: from which if ye keep yourselves, ye shall do well. Fare ye well.*
³⁰ *So when they were dismissed, they came to Antioch: and when they had gathered the multitude together, they delivered the epistle:*
³¹ *Which when they had read, they rejoiced for the consolation.*
³² *And Judas and Silas, being prophets also themselves, exhorted the brethren with many words, and confirmed them.*
³³ *And after they had tarried there a space, they were let go in peace from the brethren unto the apostles*

MATTHEW 6:23-25 KING JAMES VERSION (KJV)
²³ *But if thine eye be evil, thy whole body shall be full of darkness. If therefore the light that is in thee be darkness, how great is that darkness!*
²⁴ *No man can serve two masters: for either he will hate the one, and love the other; or else he will hold to the one, and despise the other. Ye cannot serve God and mammon.*
²⁵ *Therefore I say unto you, Take no thought for your life, what ye shall eat, or what ye shall drink; nor yet for your body, what ye shall put on. Is not the life more than meat, and the body than raiment?*

This scripture applies to more than money. Money is just used here because most of us value riches above all else. Jesus used to give us an example of what we value most. Here, we see the main principle He was conveying is we cannot say one thing and act out another because that which is of most value is what we will adhere to. We tend to be selfish by nature. Yes, we as Christians cannot uphold two opposing standards. We have to renounce one or the other because they are exact opposites. We see in the church today there are many who promote the fact that God wants us all to be rich because we deserve it. This has led to so much confusion in the church. Jesus pointed to the fact that we will cling to that which appeals to us. He wants us to fight and resist fleshly lusts and those actions which lead us to we serve some god other than the one True God.

We can see from this that some were not holding to studying and identifying the traps of sin, which can so easily cause men to stray from the doctrine of Christ. Instead of Christ some choose to follow those things which appealed to the flesh, (immoral sex and wonton living), and accepting the teaching of false prophets. This included some which were living a life abounding in rituals to honor idols.

Idol worshippers did all sorts of things which were evil in the sight of God. They worshiped and offered sacrifices to idols, including human sacrifices (even the killing of their children). They used prostitutes as part of their lifestyle and worship experience and excepted the guidance of sorcerers. Some, even though they had claimed to accept Jesus as their Savior, were following the things which He taught were evil, causing them to be led astray and bringing a polluted lifestyle into His church. Some were not following the promptings of the Holy Spirit, which had been provided to help them follow their conscience anew and be converted to the righteousness of God. No, they had not repented of those prior works and renounced them. Even after baptism many continued to live the same pattern in life as they did prior to baptism. Thieves continued to steal as a way to make a living and some continued the practices of their original religious beliefs. This was pointed out in Paul's letter to the Ephesians.

EPHESIANS 4:17-32 KING JAMES VERSION (KJV)

[17] This I say therefore, and testify in the Lord, that ye henceforth walk not as other Gentiles walk, in the vanity of their mind,

[18] Having the understanding darkened, being alienated from the life of God through the ignorance that is in them, because of the blindness of their heart:

[19] Who being past feeling have given themselves over unto lasciviousness, to work all uncleanness with greediness.

[20] But ye have not so learned Christ;

[21] If so be that ye have heard him, and have been taught by him, as the truth is in Jesus:

[22] That ye put off concerning the fromer conversation the old man, which is corrupt according to the deceitful lusts;

[23] And be renewed in the spirit of your mind;

[24] And that ye put on the new man, which after God is created in righteousness and true holiness.

[25] Wherefore putting away lying, speak every man truth with his neighbour: for we are members one of another.

[26] Be ye angry, and sin not: let not the sun go down upon your wrath:

[27] Neither give place to the devil.

²⁸ *Let him that stole steal no more: but rather let him labour, working with his hands the thing which is good, that he may have to give to him that needeth.*
²⁹ *Let no corrupt communication proceed out of your mouth, but that which is good to the use of edifying, that it may minister grace unto the hearers.*
³⁰ *And grieve not the holy Spirit of God, whereby ye are sealed unto the day of redemption.*
³¹ *Let all bitterness, and wrath, and anger, and clamour, and evil speaking, be put away from you, with all malice:*
³² *And be ye kind one to another, tenderhearted, forgiving one another, even as God for Christ's sake hath forgiven you.*

The apostle Paul pointed out that some were only coming into the fellowship for what they could gain, while others were being led by the devil to claim falsely that they were truly repenting of their past life. Some may not have genuinely known that they were sinning in keeping these practices, while others felt because Jesus will forgive all sin, they could continue as they had in the past. Some were doing what they did in the past and treated Jesus as if they were adding another idol to their chest to have all their bases covered. It is not much different in the church today. In the beginning of our church many came from different sects which had adhered to beliefs and practices which were not of God. Today, many come with what their momma or daddy said and taught and other ideas that they hold as sacred, which are not. They want these imperfect beliefs and practices to be added to the acts God instituted as His righteousness. Many of these past practices included things such as polygamy, fornication, sorcery and other practices which God has forbade and which is not part of His teaching which are the righteous acts established by God. God calls us to perfection which will require being separated from the things of the past and being brought into the light of His truth. As scripture tells us, we now know in part but when that is perfect is come all these old things will be cast aside.

1 CORINTHIANS 15:31-37 AMPLIFIED BIBLE (AMP)
³¹ *I assure you, believers, by the pride which I have in you in [your union with] Christ Jesus our Lord, I die daily [I face death and die to self].*
³² *What good has it done me if, [merely] from a human point of view, I [a]fought with wild animals at Ephesus? If the dead are not*

raised [at all], let us eat and drink [enjoying ourselves now], for tomorrow we die.

³³ Do not be deceived: [b]"Bad company corrupts good morals."

³⁴ Be sober-minded [be sensible, wake up from your spiritual stupor] as you ought, and stop sinning; for some [of you] have no knowledge of God [you are disgracefully ignorant of Him, and ignore His truths]. I say this to your shame.

³⁵ But someone will say, "How are the dead raised? And with what kind of body will they come?"

³⁶ You fool! Every time you plant seed you sow something that does not come to life [germinating, springing up and growing] unless it first dies.

³⁷ The seed you sow is not the body (the plant) which it is going to become, but it is a bare seed, perhaps of wheat or some other grain.

Footnotes:

1 Corinthians 15:32 This may refer figuratively to the furious crowd that rose up against Paul in Ephesus, rather than to literal animals (Acts 19:23-41).

1 Corinthians 15:33 Paul quotes this one verse maxim from the writings of the Greek dramatist Menander (342-291 b.c.). "Bad company" in this case undoubtedly refers to the teachers who were denying the truth of the resurrection.

Jesus was telling them how each who accepted His rebuke (which was a wakeup call to righteous living) would gain so much more. He reminds them of how manna from heaven sustained Israel when they were in the desert and how He changed the name of those which accepted the call to repentance. Just as Abram's name was changed to Abraham, Sarai's name was changed to Sarah, and Jacob's name was changed to Israel. Jesus changed their names to represent what God would make them into as they accepted His guidance to follow Him and abandon their old life and accept His new life by following His Spirit. He wants will do the same for us all one day.

Some really never understood the commitment that they were making and that they needed to allow God to transform them. This new name is representative of the new reborn life they were being transformed into by work of the Holy Spirit. This is the conversion we as truly repentant Christians will receive by the power of the Holy Spirit living in us.

GENESIS 17:4-6 AMPLIFIED BIBLE (AMP)
⁴ "As for Me, behold, My covenant is with you,

And [as a result] you shall be the father of many nations.
⁵ "No longer shall your name be Abram (exalted father),
But your name shall be Abraham (father of a multitude);
For I will make you the father of many nations.
⁶ I will make you exceedingly fruitful, and I will make nations of you, and [a]kings will come from you.

Footnotes:
Genesis 17:6 This prophecy and promise has been literally fulfilled countless times—for example, by all of the kings of Israel and Judah.

GENESIS 17:14-16 KING JAMES VERSION (KJV)

¹⁴ And the uncircumcised man child whose flesh of his foreskin is not circumcised, that soul shall be cut off from his people; he hath broken my covenant.

¹⁵ And God said unto Abraham, As for Sarai thy wife, thou shalt not call her name Sarai, but Sarah shall her name be.

¹⁶ And I will bless her, and give thee a son also of her: yea, I will bless her, and she shall be a mother of nations; kings of people shall be of her.

GENESIS 32:24-32 KING JAMES VERSION (KJV)

²⁴ And Jacob was left alone; and there wrestled a man with him until the breaking of the day.

²⁵ And when he saw that he prevailed not against him, he touched the hollow of his thigh; and the hollow of Jacob's thigh was out of joint, as he wrestled with him.

²⁶ And he said, Let me go, for the day breaketh. And he said, I will not let thee go, except thou bless me.

²⁷ And he said unto him, What is thy name? And he said, Jacob.

²⁸ And he said, Thy name shall be called no more Jacob, but Israel: for as a prince hast thou power with God and with men, and hast prevailed.

²⁹ And Jacob asked him, and said, Tell me, I pray thee, thy name. And he said, Wherefore is it that thou dost ask after my name? And he blessed him there.

³⁰ And Jacob called the name of the place Peniel: for I have seen God face to face, and my life is preserved.

³¹ And as he passed over Penuel the sun rose upon him, and he halted upon his thigh.

³² Therefore the children of Israel eat not of the sinew which shrank, which is upon the hollow of the thigh, unto this day: because he touched the hollow of Jacob's thigh in the sinew that shrank.

As you see, He was providing them insight into what they could gain if they abandoned the old life and accepted the transforming work of the Holy Spirit. He used the miracle of His sustaining grace as a promise of what could lie ahead if they repented.

We can also see Jesus had recognized the martyrdom of one of their group. We see that they understood the depth of commitment which they were facing. They understood that the tribulations which they were faced with could lead to death in this life and that eternal life is the ultimate goal. They already had an understanding that part of being a follower of Christ meant they were going to face tribulation in this life. The degree of that tribulation had been defined in the life of one member already. So not only were they facing tribulation from external sources, they also had tribulation from within the group itself. Each of these was identified by Jesus.

We can also gather from what is being said about Jewish persecution and manna that this group was made up of mostly Jewish converts, otherwise these references would not have had much impact on gentiles. Jesus has provided sustaining manna in the form of the Holy Spirit.

Summary

So, what is to be gained from this portion of this prophecy?

1. Christ expects new converts to come just as they are but to repent and start anew. We are to come as we are with the desire for His conversion within us. We have the Holy Spirit to work this conversion work in us.
2. Our first duty as a Christian is to seek the kingdom of God and His righteousness and allow the Holy Spirit to transform us into His image.
3. The acts of sorcery, sexual immorality in any form, idol worship, sacrifices to idols, and living a lifestyle of sin are not acceptable.
4. We cannot serve two masters. If we continue to cling to our old way of life we are in peril. These old ways will hinder the work of the Church. This includes following prevailing social norms which haven't been instituted by Christ. We are to leave behind the imperfect past.

5. We have to renounce the old sinful self to allow the work of the Holy Spirit to change us.
6. Jesus is willing to work in us if we allow Him to do this. It is the inner self which has to be changed into His likeness if we allow this to occur.
7. We have to give the Holy Spirit permission to change our spirit to match that of Jesus.
8. We cannot continue in the old way of life with its ideas and be acceptable to Christ. We are to recognize in ourselves the polluted and evil practices of the past if we are to be acceptable to Him.
9. Jesus can provide all that is needed for us to change and will provide a new personality, which is indicated by a new name.
10. We need to teach and learn the aspects of a new life in Christ and what to expect as a result.
11. Many have been baptized unto repentance but have not received the gift of the Holy Spirit which regenerates our inner man. Nor can we have an understanding of eternal life without the Holy Spirit in them.
12. Tribulation is to be expected in our life as Christians.

Chapter 6

Prophecy to the Church in Thyatira

REVELATION 2:18-29 KING JAMES VERSION (KJV)
[18] And unto the angel of the Church in Thyatira write; These things saith the Son of God, who hath his eyes like unto a flame of fire, and his feet are like fine brass;
[19] I know thy works, and charity, and service, and faith, and thy patience, and thy works; and the last to be more than the first.
[20] Notwithstanding I have a few things against thee, because thou sufferest that woman Jezebel, which calleth herself a prophetess, to teach and to seduce my servants to commit fornication, and to eat things sacrificed unto idols.
[21] And I gave her space to repent of her fornication; and she repented not.
[22] Behold, I will cast her into a bed, and them that commit adultery with her into great tribulation, except they repent of their deeds.
[23] And I will kill her children with death; and all the Churches shall know that I am he which searcheth the reins and hearts: and I will give unto every one of you according to your works.
[24] But unto you I say, and unto the rest in Thyatira, as many as have not this doctrine, and which have not known the depths of Satan, as they speak; I will put upon you none other burden.
[25] But that which ye have already hold fast till I come.
[26] And he that overcometh, and keepeth my works unto the end, to him will I give power over the nations:
[27] And he shall rule them with a rod of iron; as the vessels of a potter shall they be broken to shivers: even as I received of my Father.
[28] And I will give him the morning star.

> **²⁹ He that hath an ear, let him hear what the Spirit saith unto the Churches.**

Again, I am wowed by the way Jesus addresses His people. He does not sugar coat what he sees and is most straight forward in His expectations. He specifies the blessings and curses which each segment in this group faces. From the prophecy above we see there are two segments in this group which being presented before us. One is the faithful who had accepted the rejuvenating work of the Holy Spirit, and then there were those who had not allowed the transforming work of Jesus to work in them. Again, we find in the Church those who represent a false and evil spirit at work among those who were unrepentant. He loves them both enough to point out areas they need to correct and areas which they deserve to be praised for.

In each of the prophecies to each of the churches, He introduces Himself using different images of Himself. These images are pictorials of His character traits He wants emphasized to each group. This is because in each case, there are different parts of His attributes which are needed to get their attention. He portrayed attributes in Himself in a way that they could easily understand.

Here again is the phrase "I am that I am" coming into focus. To this church He represents Let's examine this imagery. He portrays His eyes as being like those of flame. On the day of Pentecost, the Holy Spirit appeared to the group in the room as tongues of fire. This is symbolic of how fire purifies. The work of the Holy Spirit is to purify us as we allow it. The flaming eyes are also representative of how he is able to scrutinize each thought and action. He is relating to them as though they are passing through the fiery furnace, to separate the chaff (the undesirable) from the desired pure ore of gold which is identified by His true disciples. His eyes were a purifying fire which was able to discern between good and evil and determine which is operating. Then there are His feet of brass which show that He. He is something a substantial solid foundation which they can depend to be right. Not only were they brass but a burnished brass which was as pure as could be produced. A shiny surface meant to get your attention. Sandaled feet were dirty until washed. His feet not only were washed and clean, but pure and Holy. Remember, the pegs which supported the tabernacle which was carried through the desert were also made of brass. This symbolized He was their support which stabilized them and secured them during all manner of storms in life.

So, let's consider each portion of this group separately. First, there was the faithful group which had been converted to the new life in Christ. He identified that they had been demonstrating a transformed spirit and personality. He identified that they possessed the same spirit and image as He did when He was here; they acted in all things with charity (God's love). He recognized how they were faithful and the service which they were performing and finally, he mentions the works at last being greater than the works at first. The order in which they are presented is very important.

The love of God which they shared is necessary to perform anything to the glory of God and to do as He would do. This is a vital aspect of the rejuvenating work of the Holy Spirit. It is the first step in emulating anything that God does. In order for us to follow what He does, it must be done out of His type of love, which is pure and holy. This is How we are all to honor God, by doing all things purely in love to glorify Him. This personifies Him as the source of all goodness.

1 CORINTHIANS 13:2-13 KING JAMES VERSION (KJV)

² And though I have the gift of prophecy, and understand all mysteries, and all knowledge; and though I have all faith, so that I could remove mountains, and have not charity, I am nothing.

³ And though I bestow all my goods to feed the poor, and though I give my body to be burned, and have not charity, it profiteth me nothing.

⁴ Charity suffereth long, and is kind; charity envieth not; charity vaunteth not itself, is not puffed up,

⁵ Doth not behave itself unseemly, seeketh not her own, is not easily provoked, thinketh no evil;

⁶ Rejoiceth not in iniquity, but rejoiceth in the truth;

⁷ Beareth all things, believeth all things, hopeth all things, endureth all things.

⁸ Charity never faileth: but whether there be prophecies, they shall fail; whether there be tongues, they shall cease; whether there be knowledge, it shall vanish away.

⁹ For we know in part, and we prophesy in part.

¹⁰ But when that which is perfect is come, then that which is in part shall be done away.

> *¹¹ When I was a child, I spake as a child, I understood as a child, I thought as a child: but when I became a man, I put away childish things.*
> *¹² For now we see through a glass, darkly; but then face to face: now I know in part; but then shall I know even as also I am known.*
> *¹³ And now abideth faith, hope, charity, these three; but the greatest of these is charity.*

Next in the list is service. The inspiration I am led to understand is that service is the worshiping of Him and Jesus the Christ. That is, in everything we do, we should do so by prayerfully looking to be His image here on the earth glorifying Him. We then are seeking to work in accordance with His plan for mankind of establishing His kingdom here on earth. Here we see the importance that Jesus places on our surrender to Him by letting go of the old life and allowing the Holy Spirit to transform us into His image, here on this earth. It is a vital step in being able to please Him and is necessary to be a true disciple in His service. He wants us to become with each other and one with Him. He can say so much in a word and how it is used. That is what is lacking in the walk of the everyday Christian today. Many have been lulled into inactivity by the sermons which they hear that draws them to place their lustful desires above the pure love of God and of our fellow man. Therefore, the word "service" today is mute in the church. We don't get it. We have not seen the need for it. When we do many things will change. To us, service is just attending Church and doing something nice for those less fortunate than us. **_No!_** This is not what Jesus wants or what we need. Not many offer themselves in complete surrender to Him and His work in them. Here is the difference in the Church at Pentecost in scripture and the reality of the Church today. It is our lack of service which is most outstanding. We do a lot of what man considers good things, but these, without service (the love of and for the glory of God), mean nothing. Service is the actual ability to worship Him in spirit and truth, which is expected in all who are called by His name. We have demeaned the term service and identified it as our duty to attend Church or our duty to be a nice person. That is why scripture says we are to be constantly drawn out in prayer. That is, we are to be in constant unison with the Father and the Son. All that we do to honor and praise God is a prayer to Him.

> **ROMANS 12:1-3 KING JAMES VERSION (KJV)**
> ¹ I beseech you therefore, brethren, by the mercies of God, that ye present your bodies a living sacrifice, holy, acceptable unto God, which is your reasonable service.
> ² And be not conformed to this world: but be ye transformed by the renewing of your mind, that ye may prove what is that good, and acceptable, and perfect, will of God.
> ³ For I say, through the grace given unto me, to every man that is among you, not to think of himself more highly than he ought to think; but to think soberly, according as God hath dealt to every man the measure of faith.
>
> **TITUS 2:11-15 KING JAMES VERSION (KJV)**
> ¹¹ For the grace of God that bringeth salvation hath appeared to all men,
> ¹² Teaching us that, denying ungodliness and worldly lusts, we should live soberly, righteously, and godly, in this present world;
> ¹³ Looking for that blessed hope, and the glorious appearing of the great God and our Saviour Jesus Christ;
> ¹⁴ Who gave himself for us, that he might redeem us from all iniquity, and purify unto himself a peculiar people, zealous of good works.
> ¹⁵ These things speak, and exhort, and rebuke with all authority. Let no man despise thee.

Next comes faith, which is the gift provided to every true believer which causes us to respond to His invitation of a new life in Him here on this earth. You can see how Jesus puts this in sequence. There is a step by step process which occurs in the life of the believer which leads to this point. Here Jesus gives us a heads up on how it should work. Until we reach the spiritual level that God demands, we can't be entrusted with the level of faith to perform and receive the ability to have our prayers and request to be done correctly. We saw an abundance of the gifts of the Spirit in the post Pentecost followers and we have seen these diminish over the years. It is His spiritual power which identifies us as true believers then and now. There were those who were willing to pay Peter to receive the Gifts of the Spirit which he demonstrated. It is the presence of these spiritual powers at work which identifies us as true believers then and now. Yes, the gifts are still in effect and can be more abundantly practiced when there are people willing to submit to the conversion work of the Holy Spirit. But remember that the devil, is bestowing powers on His followers just as

God does for us. The difference is that the powers of God glorify Him and Jesus by producing good works unto peace and eternal life. The works of the devil result in evil, doubt, destruction suffering, turmoil and untimely to eternal death.

ACTS 8:1-25 KING JAMES VERSION (KJV)

⁸ And Saul was consenting unto his death. And at that time there was a great persecution against the Church which was at Jerusalem; and they were all scattered abroad throughout the regions of Judaea and Samaria, except the apostles.

² And devout men carried Stephen to his burial, and made great lamentation over him.

³ As for Saul, he made havock of the Church, entering into every house, and haling men and women committed them to prison.

⁴ Therefore they that were scattered abroad went every where preaching the word.

⁵ Then Philip went down to the city of Samaria, and preached Christ unto them.

⁶ And the people with one accord gave heed unto those things which Philip spake, hearing and seeing the miracles which he did.

⁷ For unclean spirits, crying with loud voice, came out of many that were possessed with them: and many taken with palsies, and that were lame, were healed.

⁸ And there was great joy in that city.

⁹ But there was a certain man, called Simon, which beforetime in the same city used sorcery, and bewitched the people of Samaria, giving out that himself was some great one:

¹⁰ To whom they all gave heed, from the least to the greatest, saying, This man is the great power of God.

¹¹ And to him they had regard, because that of long time he had bewitched them with sorceries.

¹² But when they believed Philip preaching the things concerning the kingdom of God, and the name of Jesus Christ, they were baptized, both men and women.

¹³ Then Simon himself believed also: and when he was baptized, he continued with Philip, and wondered, beholding the miracles and signs which were done.

¹⁴ Now when the apostles which were at Jerusalem heard that Samaria had received the word of God, they sent unto them Peter and John:

¹⁵ Who, when they were come down, prayed for them, that they might receive the Holy Ghost:

> [16] *(For as yet he was fallen upon none of them: only they were baptized in the name of the Lord Jesus.)*
> [17] *Then laid they their hands on them, and they received the Holy Ghost.*
> [18] *And when Simon saw that through laying on of the apostles' hands the Holy Ghost was given, he offered them money,*
> [19] *Saying, Give me also this power, that on whomsoever I lay hands, he may receive the Holy Ghost.*
> [20] *But Peter said unto him, Thy money perish with thee, because thou hast thought that the gift of God may be purchased with money.*
> [21] *Thou hast neither part nor lot in this matter: for thy heart is not right in the sight of God.*
> [22] *Repent therefore of this thy wickedness, and pray God, if perhaps the thought of thine heart may be forgiven thee.*
> [23] *For I perceive that thou art in the gall of bitterness, and in the bond of iniquity.*
> [24] *Then answered Simon, and said, Pray ye to the Lord for me, that none of these things which ye have spoken come upon me.*
> [25] *And they, when they had testified and preached the word of the Lord, returned to Jerusalem, and preached the gospel in many villages of the Samaritans.*

It is pointed out that sorcerers and magicians demonstrate acts that get our attention and because of the feats which they are able to perform, many places them on a pedestal. Yes, there are powers at work we can't explain or duplicate because the source for them resides in an evil power and His followers. We don't want to admit this is real, but it is. Today we identify this as superstition rather than reality because we are guided by what we call the principles of science and our intelligence rather than accept the fact of a real devil and a real God (a spiritual existence beyond our sight). Our perceptions are based on our senses and if we can't touch, see, or taste, the experience or can't prove it by scientific examination or our interpretation of physical evidence for it, we don't accept it. We are provided evidence of these in scripture by the magicians in Pharaoh's court and Balaam and the sorcerers that Paul and others faced. These are mentioned over and over again in scripture, but we dismiss these as fables or fairy tales or allegory. We are enthralled by modern day magicians, most of whom perform feats which are just tricks or illusions, but there are true magicians who receive power from Satan. There are also sorcerers in this day and time at work who are able to receive power from Satan. Today we might call them mediums or spiritual advisors. We try dismiss this as trickery. Some of it is but, some of it is not. We will see a resurgence of this in the anti-Christ and some of His predecessors. It is Satan using a counterfeit of the power of the Spirit which is expressed as healing, speaking in tongues, prophecy and more. He is able to impart special abilities to His followers just as God does, but those of God carry His power which can overcome those of the devil. The power of God is much greater. We will have to grasp the concept that there is a spiritual dimension and not just the physical one bound by time and space as we know it. Einstein was on the verge of proving it with his theory of relativity. Consider this scripture.

>   EXODUS 7:9-12 KING JAMES VERSION (KJV)
>
> [9] When Pharaoh shall speak unto you, saying, Shew a miracle for you: then thou shalt say unto Aaron, Take thy rod, and cast it before Pharaoh, and it shall become a serpent.
>
> [10] And Moses and Aaron went in unto Pharaoh, and they did so as the Lord had commanded: and Aaron cast down his rod before Pharaoh, and before his servants, and it became a serpent.
>
> [11] Then Pharaoh also called the wise men and the sorcerers: now the magicians of Egypt, they also did in like manner with their enchantments.
>
> [12] For they cast down every man his rod, and they became serpents: but Aaron's rod swallowed up their rods.
>
>   ACTS 13:5-7 KING JAMES VERSION (KJV)
>
> [5] And when they were at Salamis, they preached the word of God in the synagogues of the Jews: and they had also John to their minister.
>
> [6] And when they had gone through the isle unto Paphos, they found a certain sorcerer, a false prophet, a Jew, whose name was Barjesus:
>
> [7] Which was with the deputy of the country, Sergius Paulus, a prudent man; who called for Barnabas and Saul, and desired to hear the word of God.

Of course, many today are taught not to believe the exodus in Genesis actually, occurred so they are unwilling to accept this reference. Nor do they want to accept that God prophesied the reestablishment of the nation of Israel. Yet we keep looking for the battle of Armageddon and the rapture. Pray that the Lord will confirm the existence of the two realms to you and if you approach Him in faith you will receive the answer. It is more than the good feeling we have when we say we can feel the good spirit or we are in His presence. I have experienced both realms and I tell you that heaven is best. I have seen both God and the devil. God is the best choice. The devil has a black appearance which is so dark that light cannot penetrate him. Yet some accept him as an angel of light. God is the source of light and truth. Please excuse my wandering but in my spirit, I feel this must be said.

Next, Jesus lists their patience, which as stated before is a virtue we as Christians need to inherit. It is the fact not all His promises will be fulfilled at once but they will be done in due time. This is also a call to pay attention to their perseverance which was indicated by the fact they were to be willing to endure until the end, or mortal death. It is a concept that we in modern America don't really seem to grasp. Our psyche is based on immediate gratification and pleasure. Christians in America for the most part have not had to endure the hardships those in Roman times did. Well maybe I should mention those who lynch and perform all manner of atrocities to those who are not of their race and it goes unreported and many times are ignored by those in the Church. It happens here but many do not feel the impact or choose to accept it as such. We accept violence to others as long it does not impact our family or when it is portrayed in a way in that we can accept as 'just' retribution. We allow ourselves to be blind to these unrighteous acts and choose to support them by hiding behind the acts of privilege by virtue of our race or position in life by the fact that we have been convinced by others that they deserve what they get. That which is the worst of all is our unwillingness to stand up against wrongs (our silence). We are armed to the teeth and vow to defend ourselves and our families against an enemy yet we don't see that all members of Christ no matter what race or what nationality are our brother and sister and deserve to be treated in Godly love. It is the choice we make to kill or be killed. Or as we are told in scripture, we live by the statement ***"those who live by the sword will die by sword". This has a two-edged meaning. Those who live by the word of God will die by it or those live by might will die as a result of it. Really thing about this.***

Patience is the willingness to live by God's authority and no other. It is a choice to love God without reservation and trust Him with our very eternal existence. It is the virtue to live by and endure the threats of unchristian beliefs and actions unto mortal death if it is so required. It is the willingness to trust that God will justly punish all at the end. It is the recognition that He stands with us through everything and that we have the strength to endure to the end. Recall how you have weathered so many storms in this life already and that you made it. Yes, you may have a few scars but with His help you survived. He is the salve which will heal all wounds incurred in as His here on this earth.

Patience is the opposite of revenge and forgiveness is the first step needed to receive it. It is our love of God and our fellow man which makes up our patience.

2 CHRONICLES 5:10-14 KING JAMES VERSION (KJV)

[10] There was nothing in the ark save the two tables which Moses put therein at Horeb, when the Lord made a covenant with the children of Israel, when they came out of Egypt.

[11] And it came to pass, when the priests were come out of the holy place: (for all the priests that were present were sanctified, and did not then wait by course:

[12] Also the Levites which were the singers, all of them of Asaph, of Heman, of Jeduthun, with their sons and their brethren, being arrayed in white linen, having cymbals and psalteries and harps, stood at the east end of the altar, and with them an hundred and twenty priests sounding with trumpets:)

[13] It came even to pass, as the trumpeters and singers were as one, to make one sound to be heard in praising and thanking the Lord; and when they lifted up their voice with the trumpets and cymbals and instruments of musick, and praised the Lord, saying, For he is good; for his mercy endureth for ever: that then the house was filled with a cloud, even the house of the Lord;

[14] So that the priests could not stand to minister by reason of the cloud: for the glory of the Lord had filled the house of God.

Then comes the statement about the works which they were performing and how those which occurred later were greater than those they did at first. I am led to understand that the works they performed now are more out of love than duty. They performed works at first by following learned procedures but later they began performing out of Godly love for their brothers and sisters and out of love for God and for His glory, which is vital in our walk as Christians.

PSALM 117:1-2 KING JAMES VERSION(KJV)

[1] O praise the Lord, all ye nations: praise him, all ye people.

> ² *For his merciful kindness is great toward us: and the truth of the Lord endureth for ever. Praise ye the Lord.*
> **MATTHEW 10:21-23 AMPLIFIED BIBLE**
> ²¹ *"Brother will betray brother to death, and the father his child; and children will rise up and rebel against their parents and cause them to be put death.*
> ²² *And you will be hated by everyone because of [your association with] My name, but it is the one who has patiently persevered and endured to the end who will be saved.*
> ²³ *"When they persecute you in one city [because of your faith in Me], flee to the next; for I assure you and most solemnly say to you, you will not finish going through all the cities of Israel before the Son of Man comes.*

As I stated earlier, He notes the works were greater in the latest part of their walk. Now works can designate the performance of acts toward others or it can refer to the spirit in which things are undertaken or a combination of the two. In this case, it is the fact that they had grown spiritually which indicates Jesus is referring to the fact that now in performing their actions, there was a pleasing change which was occurring. Not only were they doing good works but now those works were being performed out the love of God in their hearts. What had happened was they had allowed the Holy Spirit to bring about a change in their spirit which had resulted in the transformation to be more like Jesus. This is what is to occur in us all.

He then addresses the second group in this Church. It was a group who were being led astray by a self-proclaimed prophetess named Jezebel. Now this is not the one listed in the Old Testament. Here, we also see a pattern that has emerged. It is common in most churches for fakes and those who are following the devil to hold a prominent role among worshipers. This is something we need to be aware of and be ready to protect ourselves against. What this Jezebel was doing was teaching the worshipers who could easily be persuaded, to commit fornication. It does not say that she was denouncing Jesus, but that she was hiding in plain sight claiming to be sent from Him. This is a tactic still in use today which we have to be aware of. So many today claim they are prophets, which are not, and many who are eager to know the future eagerly follow them. They think listening to them will provide a way for them to outfox the devil and His plan but don't realize that he is outfoxing them and using their gullibility against them. She used her claim to be a prophet to turn many away from the true path using a disguise which they saw as real. Her followers were not equipped with the truth so they were easily swayed by a counterfeit gospel. We can easily be swayed by our lusts when we are not truly regenerated yet. We should be smart enough to know things like this are labeled as sin, but we are easily misled into thinking it is ok to sin because Jesus will forgive anything or if we are doing it "out of love". **_Wrong!_** We also have been misled to believe that because we don't see the immediate repercussions from our choices, we have escaped the punishment. **_Not So!_**

2 TIMOTHY 4:2-4 KING JAMES VERSION (KJV)
² Preach the word; be instant in season, out of season; reprove, rebuke, exhort with all long suffering and doctrine.
³ For the time will come when they will not endure sound doctrine; but after their own lusts shall they heap to themselves teachers, having itching ears;
⁴ And they shall turn away their ears from the truth, and shall be turned unto fables.

There is a point here to recognize. There are many who claim they are called of God but are not. We can usually identify this by the fact they claim it is *their* ministry and not the ministry of Jesus who was raised from the dead. They teach things which appeal to the lusts of men, but do not express the need for the righteousness of God. They use glowing words and produce performances which appeal to men, but do not glorify God. They try to speak as an authority and have many pamphlets and other documents printed to prove their point. They don't live in accordance with the gospel they preach. They accumulate riches for their glory and not to glorify God. They brag about how good God has been to them by providing all these wonderful, worldly possessions and yet, will not share their wealth. They may say they tithe but that is not based on love but it is a ploy. They seem to all want to accumulate as much as they can only to consume it on their own lusts. They need more and more for their ministry, not God's work. They convince their followers that God wants us all to be rich here on this earth, and to live in the lap of luxury and claim as much as we can for ourselves, and the rest of the world doesn't count. They teach that the possessions of the sinful rich are theirs and one day they will get it all. They emphasize that we are endowed by God to have all the riches of the world and we need to get it now.

I am led to point out that the teaching of Jezebel was not sexual in nature but they were being convinced to accept other gods. This is confirmed in the next statement in which Jesus points to the fact they were eating food sacrificed to idols. The fact that the food is sacrificed by them to idols indicates they had returned to worshiping idols. This was what they were called to repent of on the day of their commitment to Christ. Examples of this concept are statements made in scripture which equate worshipping other gods as fornication or adultery or as whoring after other gods. Now it could also include sexual immorality, but here the main issue is that they were being taught that it was OK to worship other gods. If the main object of her teaching was sexual immorality then Jesus would have stated it as such. They had been taught in the beginning that idols were nothing but wood or stone with no power, but Jezebel had presented this in ways which were appealing. This is the same thing that happened while Moses went up on the mountain to meet God. The group down below built a golden calf to worship and partied with it. Here are some scriptures which confirm this.

> **2 CHRONICLES 21:10-17 KING JAMES VERSION (KJV)**
> *¹⁰ So the Edomites revolted from under the hand of Judah unto this day. The same time also did Libnah revolt from under his hand; because he had forsaken the Lord God of his fathers.*
> *¹¹ Moreover he made high places in the mountains of Judah and caused the inhabitants of Jerusalem to commit fornication, and compelled Judah thereto.*
> *¹² And there came a writing to him from Elijah the prophet, saying, Thus saith the Lord God of David thy father, Because thou hast not walked in the ways of Jehoshaphat thy father, nor in the ways of Asa king of Judah,*
> *¹³ But hast walked in the way of the kings of Israel, and hast made Judah and the inhabitants of Jerusalem to go a whoring, like to the whoredoms of the house of Ahab, and also hast slain thy brethren of thy father's house, which were better than thyself:*
> *¹⁴ Behold, with a great plague will the Lord smite thy people, and thy children, and thy wives, and all thy goods:*
> *¹⁵ And thou shalt have great sickness by disease of thy bowels, until thy bowels fall out by reason of the sickness day by day.*

¹⁶ Moreover the Lord stirred up against Jehoram the spirit of the Philistines, and of the Arabians, that were near the Ethiopians:
¹⁷ And they came up into Judah, and brake into it, and carried away all the substance that was found in the king's house, and his sons also, and his wives; so that there was never a son left him, save Jehoahaz, the youngest of his sons.

EZEKIEL 16:28-30 KING JAMES VERSION (KJV)

²⁸ Thou hast played the whore also with the Assyrians, because thou wast unsatiable; yea, thou hast played the harlot with them, and yet couldest not be satisfied.
²⁹ Thou hast moreover multiplied thy fornication in the land of Canaan unto Chaldea; and yet thou wast not satisfied therewith.
³⁰ How weak is thine heart, saith the Lord God, seeing thou doest all these things, the work of an imperious whorish woman;

So, anyone who teaches doctrines which are the opposite of those of Jesus can be considered as leading the people to commit whoredoms. We are also told the fate of those who were committing these acts. It is stated that Jezebel and her children, (which are those who accepted her teachings), were going to be punished as an example to the rest of the believers. (I ask you to call your attention to Ananias and Sapphira in Acts chapter 5:1-15. Now Jesus also points out that He had provided time for Jezebel and her followers to see the error of their ways and when they didn't repent, He had to act. So, when we see evil practices at work and they are not stopped immediately, we have to recognize that God still loves the evildoers and that He will provide an opportunity for them to repent. Note that, we still have a responsibility to act against such perversion. When Jesus finally sees there is no hope of their repenting without Him taking drastic action, He does what He has to do according to what His loving justice demands. This is a stark warning that sin results in death. When worshipers turn from the true God, without repenting, in some allotted period of time God responds in judgement which is painful and results in His withdrawal of His protection and Satan is allowed to have his way with them.

You see Satan does not care about treating his followers kindly. In his anger against God he wants to bring about the destruction of the human race in retribution for God's punishment of him. Satan does not reward his followers, as many are not aware. He just intensifies their suffering and pain. Just as Balaam knew that if the nation of Israel accepted harlots and committed fornication with them and other gods that God out of His justice would have to punish them.

> **1 CORINTHIANS 10:5-15 KING JAMES VERSION (KJV)**
> *⁵ But with many of them God was not well pleased: for they were overthrown in the wilderness.*
> *⁶ Now these things were our examples, to the intent we should not lust after evil things, as they also lusted.*
> *⁷ Neither be ye idolaters, as were some of them; as it is written, The people sat down to eat and drink, and rose up to play.*
> *⁸ Neither let us commit fornication, as some of them committed, and fell in one day three and twenty thousand.*
> *⁹ Neither let us tempt Christ, as some of them also tempted, and were destroyed of serpents.*
> *¹⁰ Neither murmur ye, as some of them also murmured, and were destroyed of the destroyer.*
> *¹¹ Now all these things happened unto them for examples: and they are written for our admonition, upon whom the ends of the world are come.*
> *¹² Wherefore let him that thinketh he standeth take heed lest he fall.*
> *¹³ There hath no temptation taken you but such as is common to man: but God is faithful, who will not suffer you to be tempted above that ye are able; but will with the temptation also make a way to escape, that ye may be able to bear it.*
> *¹⁴ Wherefore, my dearly beloved, flee from idolatry.*
> *¹⁵ I speak as to wise men; judge ye what I say.*

Lastly, we see here that Jesus turns again to those who have not adhered to the doctrine of Jezebel and reassures His loyal followers that He will not place any other burden on them. But they still had to carry the responsibly of allowing Jezebel's teaching to continue without moving to prove it was all a lie. They, just as we, had the responsibility to identify false teaching and to call those who are doing this to repent. This is a burden they had to carry. Jesus tells them He will not place any further burden on them, but that He would take over and do what needed to be done. The knowledge that they had failed in their responsibility was enough. Can you see that He loved them enough to have them learn by their mistakes after He pointed out their errors? Sometimes we can't escape the results of our choices. His forgiveness does not always result in earthly release from the results of our sin. Some will have to live with those sexually transmitted diseases they contracted. Others will have to go to jail for the murders they committed. Though Jesus does not want to see any suffer, our suffering at times is used to demonstrate the consequences of sin. It is not that He desires our suffering but He wants others to learn the results of sin. This is another reason we are to be patient in this life because the benefits which we receive through Jesus' sacrifice will not always be evident at this time. Sometimes we glorify God by allowing Him to demonstrate that the results of sin in this life leads to pain and suffering.

He closes by stating additional powers which they will receive only after they have successfully ended their earthly existence. This is important in that these abilities will only be received at the end of their stay here and only when they are with Him will these powers be granted. When with Him in glory, they will be converted to be perfect, just as He is perfect. Then they will have the ability to judge justly. They will love with a perfect love and disseminate justice with the same love as He does, which will cause them to be able to break down the evil empires into pieces though the word of their testimony. This means they will be able to show all that was evil and dismantle the powers they had to bring suffering and to subvert the work of the Lord. These powers will not be presented here on this earth but only when they are with Him. Then they will share in His glory. He will provide them the morning star, which is Jesus Himself.

As it is always the case, He ends with the statement that those who so choose can understand the meaning and respond to His message.

Summary

There is a lot to be learned from this group. We can see there is just judgement allotted, and how Jesus works in the life of His Church, and the standards which He sets and requires of us. Here is what we should gain as insights from this prophetic utterance.
1. Jesus loves us enough to point out what it is we are doing both right and wrong. Out of His love He will execute judgement as needed
2. Jesus is whatever the Church needs as it is required.

3. We as Christians are to develop by the power of the Holy Spirit certain things.
    a. It takes a work of the Holy Spirit to produce true Godly love in us.
    b. It takes a work of the Spirit to truly work the change in us to become one with Him and all our brothers and sisters.
    c. It takes the work of the Spirit to cause the change to occur just as we can as John was in the Spirit and able to receive the word of the Lord (one with the Spirit as He was when this prophecy was given)
    d. We have to completely surrender ourselves (repent of all sin) to Him which is the service we are called to perform. This means repenting of all our past sins and allowing the Holy Spirit to transform us into the image of Christ so that we become one with Him and our brothers and sisters in Christ.
    e. Patience is actually trusting in love that God is true to His promises and that the things we are going through are being allowed to glorify God. It is a virtue which can only be received by the work of the Holy Spirit. It is more than can be explained in human terms. It is a spiritual place not many have experienced.
4. Then there is faith. This is a process of trust in God allotted to us as we grow in submitting ourselves in service to God.
    a. Each one of His followers is provided a gift of faith.
    b. He cannot entrust much to those who are not trustworthy to act as He acts and love as He loves.
    c. As we grow in faith of Him, He will entrust more of His power to us.
5. As we are converted from doing things from a fleshly perspective to doing things in Godly love for the glory of God, the results of what we do change in the same relationship.
    a. Works done out of love for God and to his glory for our fellow saints are pleasing to Jesus and are seen as "greater" to Him than those we do out of duty or responsibility. This is what we are to seek through Him by the power of the Holy Spirit.

6. We have to be on guard against and respond to false teachers with the truth and prove them as liars. We do this through the power of the Spirit in love within.
    a. We have to know false teachings and recognize when Satan is working through someone.
    b. This takes not only knowledge but courage to act.
    c. We are not to sit back and allow anything impure to interrupt the work of God.
7. Just as Jesus calls us to repent from serving other gods and following false teachers. It is our role to call others, especially in the Church to repent from such practices.
    a. People can easily be led to return to their old ways if it is presented in the right way.
    b. People are gullible and will gravitate to those things which appeal to the lusts of their flesh. If it appeals to my sensual-self then I can be attracted to accept it.
8. Jesus will allow the sinful to exist in the Church for a time which to us seems as acceptance but He is only allotting time for the sinners to repent and for us to expose their sin.
9. Jesus will punish the sinful even unto death if required. It is done openly so that others may understand what the consequences of sin are.
10. Even though Jesus will forgive all things when we repent, there are times when He will allow us to experience the consequences of our sin as a lesson for others.
11. When we are with Him, we will be converted to be perfect as He is and we will receive power to overcome even empires of evil and expose and dismantle their power over man.

CHAPTER 7

Prophecy to the Church in Sardis

> **REVELATION 3:1-6 KING JAMES VERSION (KJV)**
> *¹ And unto the angel of the Church in Sardis write; These things saith he that hath the seven Spirits of God, and the seven stars; I know thy works, that thou hast a name that thou livest, and art dead.*
> *² Be watchful, and strengthen the things which remain, that are ready to die: for I have not found thy works perfect before God.*
> *³ Remember therefore how thou hast received and heard, and hold fast, and repent. If therefore thou shalt not watch, I will come on thee as a thief, and thou shalt not know what hour I will come upon thee.*
> *⁴ Thou hast a few names even in Sardis which have not defiled their garments; and they shall walk with me in white: for they are worthy.*
> *⁵ He that overcometh, the same shall be clothed in white raiment; and I will not blot out his name out of the book of life, but I will confess his name before my Father, and before his angels.*
> *⁶ He that hath an ear, let him hear what the Spirit saith unto the Churches.*

This is a profound message for all time. Jesus represents Himself as the one who is holding the seven spirits and the seven stars. He is using this image to reinforce the fact that they are under His authority and in His control. The same goes for the image of the image of the seven spirits, which represents the seven Churches in this region. He is relating that their authority and power emanates from and originates in Him. Without Him they have no power or authority and essentially no life. Jesus is the source of that which brings life and the connection with Him is all they have that will save them. Jesus warns them to be vigilant for there is no indication of when their opportunity here will end.

> **LUKE 21:33-35 AMPLIFIED BIBLE**
> **³³ Heaven and earth will pass away, but My words will not pass away.**
> **³⁴ "But be on guard, so that your hearts are not weighed down and depressed with the giddiness of debauchery and the nausea of self-indulgence and the worldly worries of life, and then that day [when the Messiah returns] will not come on you suddenly like a trap;**
> **³⁵ for it will come upon all those who live on the face of all the earth.**

Here he is providing divine guidance for their salvation. There is still a connection between Him and them which has not been completely severed. He is telling they still have a link to the Holy Spirit, which resurrect or revive the spirit with which they first connected. They had wandered and had been drawn into a state of self-indulgence and doing things which identify with worldly desires and lusts, which they were originally sought to be set free from. He is using this to signify that they were identified by a lifestyle other than the one He wanted them to live. The life they now lived provided a new name not of His choosing but that of the life-style promoted by man. Now they had chosen to be something other than His. They had succumbed to this pattern which he had freed them from yet they had returned to it. So, in His eyes they were dead just as they were before accepting His call to repentance and the rejuvenating life of the Holy Spirit. The true life which they had originally received was no longer evident in the way they lived so the dead things which men choose, rather than the eternal truths, no longer were part of their choices and existence.

Jesus is telling them there is still hope and that there is still time available for them to repent and return to the things which He has provided when they first accepted Him as their Saviour. He tells them that they each have a limited time available which only He knew. This is message for all of us. Again, the love of Jesus is being demonstrated in that He has not given up on them yet but the clock was ticking. We each have a limited time on this earth in which we have the opportunity to turn to Him. It is not given to us to know the day or time. Therefore, **_we must respond now_** while there is yet time when we are presented the opportunity for us to accept the revelation of Him in us and to glorify Him by our conduct.

The works they were doing were no longer in the spirit of Christ which is to love selflessly and for the glory of God. Even though their works may have been what men may call good, Jesus saw their works as evil because the motives behind what they were doing was not for His glory nor out of love for Him and their fellow men but for the lust of their flesh and their benefit.

He identifies there were still a few faithful remaining. He always seems to be able to reserve a few who continue to live for Him. They were those who are still holding fast to the regenerated life provided by His Spirit in them.

Here is a blockbuster. Jesus tells them that He can delete their names from the book of life, which has the names of all those who have eternal life. This is the second death that being in Him protects us from. They were one step from committing the unpardonable sin, which is once we have received the full knowledge of Jesus and having accepted it, and we reject Him again, we can no longer be forgiven ever again. Here is the answer to the once saved always saved position that some espouse. We always have the choice to reject or accept God up to a point. There are those who have accepted Christ who by the lusts of the flesh, can still be convinced that we can do whatever pleases us and Christ will forgive. We see over and over the statement in these prophecies that only those who overcome to the end will have eternal life. That period, for us, is when we die the first death which we describe as death of this mortal body. We need to be ever vigilant that we are following the Holy Spirit and the work He is called to do in us. If we do this, we are assured we will endure to the end. At that point we are sealed for evermore. If we keep fighting the Holy Spirit and His attempts to work in us, and return to the works of Satan and our old choices which we made before our knowledge of Him, we are lost forevermore. This is verified by a revelation provided to our Church years ago.

SECTION 76:4A-4F DOCTRINE & COVENANTS
[Sec 76:4a] Thus saith the Lord, concerning all those who know my power, and have been made partakers thereof, and suffered themselves, through the power of the Devil, to be overcome, and to deny the truth, and defy my power;

> *[Sec 76:4b] they are they who are the sons of perdition, of whom I say it had been better for them never to have been born;*
> *[Sec 76:4c] for they are vessels of wrath, doomed to suffer the wrath of God, with the Devil and his angels, in eternity, concerning whom I have said there is no forgiveness in this world nor in the world to come;*
> *[Sec 76:4d] having denied the Holy Spirit, after having received it, and having denied the only begotten Son of the Father; having crucified him unto themselves, and put him to an open shame:*
> *[Sec 76:4e] these are they who shall go away into the lake of fire and brimstone, with the Devil and his angels, and the only ones on whom the second death shall have any power; yea, verily, the only ones who shall not be redeemed in the due time of the Lord, after the sufferings of his wrath;*
> *[Sec 76:4f] for all the rest shall be brought forth by the resurrection of the dead, through the triumph and the glory of the Lamb, who was slain, who was in the bosom of the Father before the worlds were made.*

Summary

Jesus in addressing those in this church is providing some important information for us all. He does not provide the same details which He did to the previous Churches but speaks to the most important part of our response of His invitation which is to repent and allow the Holy Spirit to remake us in His image. A few faithful had not resisted this temptation. The others were close to the point of again rejecting Him and His work in them and had been wooed by the devil to return to their old life style. The others still had an opening to repent but the time for them to do this was fading away.

So, what can we gain from this?

1. Even where are those who continue in sin, Jesus because of His love for us, offers to help bring us back before it is too late.
2. Those who are truly His, receive authority and power from Him.
3. If the works we do, are not done to the glory of God out of Godly love and to Jesus, they don't matter. They are to Him, dead works and have no eternal value.
4. Our works are evaluated based on the intent in which they are performed. The most important one is the acceptance of Jesus

as our savior and God as the creator and source of all that is in existence. The love of God and the love of our fellow saints is to be the source of all we do.
5. We are to always approach all we do in prayer asking for help to do all for His glory.
6. When we consider that it is our choice to remain in His hands, it has to be a commitment until the end of this mortal life, wherein we are sealed to life eternal.
7. Once we have received a full knowledge of Jesus and choose to reject Him again, we no longer have the gift of eternal life and must take part in the second death. It is the unpardonable sin, or the sin against the Holy Spirit for which none can be forgiven.
8. When we return again to our selfish nature and choose to not follow that regenerated conscience within us, we become worse than we were before we accepted His forgiveness.

Chapter 8

Prophecy to the Church in Philadelphia

REVELATION 3:7-13 KING JAMES VERSION (KJV)
7 And to the angel of the Church in Philadelphia write; These things saith he that is holy, he that is true, he that hath the key of David, he that openeth, and no man shutteth; and shutteth, and no man openeth;
8 I know thy works: behold, I have set before thee an open door, and no man can shut it: for thou hast a little strength, and hast kept my word, and hast not denied my name.
9 Behold, I will make them of the synagogue of Satan, which say they are Jews, and are not, but do lie; behold, I will make them to come and worship before thy feet, and to know that I have loved thee.
10 Because thou hast kept the word of my patience, I also will keep thee from the hour of temptation, which shall come upon all the world, to try them that dwell upon the earth.
11 Behold, I come quickly: hold that fast which thou hast, that no man take thy crown.
12 Him that overcometh will I make a pillar in the temple of my God, and he shall go no more out: and I will write upon him the name of my God, and the name of the city of my God, which is new Jerusalem, which cometh down out of heaven from my God: and I will write upon him my new name.
13 He that hath an ear, let him hear what the Spirit saith unto the Churches.

Here unlike the prophecy to the other churches, Jesus does not use any part of the image presented in the opening of the vision to John. It is here He uses plain language which is more straightforward. By using plain straight forward talk, He shows that He respects that this group will understand Him being straight forward using plain language. This group was mature in Him so He was able to present them things in an adult manner. There was no need to talk about anything that they did not need to be concerned with. This group had been sealed unto Him and there was no mistaking this point.

It is also obvious that this group had a Jewish heritage which is why He speaks of His kinship to King David. Lineage is very important in Jewish belief system and here Jesus reinforces this through the mention of his kinship to King David. They understood from prophecies in the Old Testament that the Eternal King would be of the offspring of King David. He was the eternal High Priest which they had been waiting for all their lives. This is the message that Jewish worshippers have been waiting for since it was first proclaimed in scripture. He is stating that all that has been prophesied through all the past prophets in the Old Testament are now fulfilled in Him.

Jesus knows is assured they accept that He is the way, the truth, and life. In Him resides all knowledge and He is the final truth. There is no other truth other than Him and as stated in scripture, He is the eternal King of all nations. He states plainly that He has the power to admit or He that can withhold admission unto His kingdom. Using the image of a door, He is letting them know that they can have access to Him because this is His choice. It is He who has opened the way to fellowship in Him, not their own power or through their own desire, but by His. It is not their linage, but His that opens the way to the Messiah they have long looked for. Here is the message for all time. Their salvation which has been prophesied over and over again, has finally arrived. In our time we say He has placed out the welcome mat.

Here we can see that they were not many in number as He states they have little strength, but with Him they hold the needed power to overtake what they are about to face. They had insight into how he always provided victory in battle with a limited number of warriors. They understood with Him they would be victorious no matter what they had to face. It was not numbers that defined their strength, it was Jesus. All they needed was Him.

He provides an insight which is very important to the Jewish community and to us as Christians. There are many who claimed to be Jews but in reality, they were not. Jesus states they were disciples of the devil and that is where their reward is connected. He tells them they are not be concerned because they will be sustained by Him and those who are now their enemies, will be made to worship at their feet, they will not be successful in their attempts to destroy them for the power of Jesus is all that is needed to prevent this from happening. These believers will come to know that they are Christ's and have been sealed unto Him for all eternity. These false Jews can't prevent His salvation so the believers are to be patient (trust in love) and be assured that His promises will be realized.

Here He uses the image of the temple and the pillars used to support the building as them. He uses this to show them and those like them that they are the structure of the temple in the New Jerusalem, which is built in heaven, not by human effort, but the hands of God. We are told we make up His temple and just as it stated, the church was built for man, not man for the church. Man is the church, not a building or location. Here again Jesus reinforces the fact we make up His temple. We are the internal support which is the true temple of God. This is again is a reinforcement that this is a group of Jewish believers who have accepted Jesus as their savior. This is because they can identify with the temple and what it stood for. The temple was to be the habitation of God and His worshipers. We can also understand from this that the Jerusalem here on earth does not meet the standard of holiness and truth which was intended from the beginning. So, God will replace it with its namesake which is holy and full of grace and truth. Again, we find the statement which indicates God will place His name on them and that their habitation is to be with Him. Jesus referenced that "He would prepare a place for us for in His Father's House which has many mansions".

Jesus tells of an hour of temptation which the whole world must face. It is pointed out that we all are going to have temptations come our way. When the disciples asked Jesus how to pray, He included the statement of us asking God to be prevent us from being led into temptation. Evidently, we can be protected from this if we call upon

God to help us and to protect us from these temptations. We are told in scripture how temptations arise. They begin as thought based on something that appeals to us. These are things which are fleshly in nature which we can refuse if we choose. The Holy Spirit provides the strength we need to resist these temptations. Let's examine this as this is presented in scripture.

JAMES 1:1-3 KING JAMES VERSION (KJV)

¹ James, a servant of God and of the Lord Jesus Christ, to the twelve tribes which are scattered abroad, greeting.
² My brethren, count it all joy when ye fall into divers temptations;
³ Knowing this, that the trying of your faith worketh patience.

JAMES 1:13-15 KING JAMES VERSION (KJV)

¹³ Let no man say when he is tempted, I am tempted of God: for God cannot be tempted with evil, neither tempteth he any man:
¹⁴ But every man is tempted, when he is drawn away of his own lust, and enticed.
¹⁵ Then when lust hath conceived, it bringeth forth sin: and sin, when it is finished, bringeth forth death.

1 PETER 1:3-25 AMPLIFIED BIBLE (AMP)

³ Blessed [gratefully praised and adored] be the God and Father of our Lord Jesus Christ, who according to His abundant and boundless mercy has caused us to be born again [that is, to be reborn from above—spiritually transformed, renewed, and set apart for His purpose] to an ever-living hope and confident assurance through the resurrection of Jesus Christ from the dead,
⁴ [born anew] into an inheritance which is imperishable [beyond the reach of change] and undefiled and unfading, reserved in heaven for you,
⁵ who are being protected and shielded by the power of God through your faith for salvation that is ready to be revealed [for you] in the last time.
⁶ In this you rejoice greatly, even though now for a little while, if necessary, you have been distressed by various trials,
⁷ so that the genuineness of your faith, which is much more precious than gold which is perishable, even though tested and purified by fire, may be found to result in [your] praise and glory and honor at the revelation of Jesus Christ.
⁸ Though you have not seen Him, you love Him; and though you do not even see Him now, you believe and trust in Him and you greatly rejoice and delight with inexpressible and glorious joy,

⁹ receiving as the result [the outcome, the consummation] of your faith, the salvation of [a]your souls.

¹⁰ Regarding this salvation, the prophets who prophesied about the grace [of God] that was intended for you, searched carefully and inquired [about this future way of salvation],

¹¹ seeking to find out what person or what time the Spirit of Christ within them was indicating as He foretold the sufferings of Christ and the glories [destined] to follow.

¹² It was revealed to them that their services [their prophecies regarding grace] were not [meant] for themselves and their time, but for you, in these things [the death, resurrection, and glorification of Jesus Christ] which have now been told to you by those who preached the gospel to you by the [power of the] Holy Spirit [who was] sent from heaven. Into these things even the angels long to look.

¹³ So prepare your minds for action, be completely sober [in spirit— steadfast, self-disciplined, spiritually and morally alert], fix your hope completely on the grace [of God] that is coming to you when Jesus Christ is revealed.

¹⁴ [Live] as obedient children [of God]; do not be conformed to the evil desires which governed you in your ignorance [before you knew the requirements and transforming power of the good news regarding salvation].

¹⁵ But like the Holy One who called you, be holy yourselves in all your conduct [be set apart from the world by your godly character and moral courage];

¹⁶ because it is written, "You shall be holy (set apart), for I am holy."

¹⁷ If you address as Father, the One who impartially judges according to each one's work, conduct yourselves in [reverent] fear [of Him] and with profound respect for Him throughout the time of your stay on earth.

¹⁸ For you know that you were not redeemed from your useless [spiritually unproductive] way of life inherited [by tradition] from your forefathers with perishable things like silver and gold,

¹⁹ but [you were actually purchased] with precious blood, like that of a [sacrificial] lamb unblemished and spotless, the priceless blood of Christ.

²⁰ For He was [b]foreordained (foreknown) before the foundation of the world, but has appeared [publicly] in these last times for your sake

> [21] *and through Him you believe [confidently] in God [the heavenly Father], who raised Him from the dead and gave Him glory, so that your faith and hope are [centered and rest] in God.*
> [22] *Since by your obedience to the truth you have purified yourselves for a sincere love of the believers, [see that you] love one another from the heart [always unselfishly seeking the best for one another],*
> [23] *for you have been born again [that is, reborn from above— spiritually transformed, renewed, and set apart for His purpose] not of seed which is perishable but [from that which is] imperishable and immortal, that is, through the living and everlasting word of God.*
> [24] *For, "All flesh is like grass, And all its glory like the flower of grass. The grass withers And the flower falls off,*
> [25] *But the word of the Lord endures forever." And this is the word [the good news of salvation] which was preached to you.*
>
> **Footnotes:**
> *1 Peter 1:9 One early ms does not contain your.*
> *1 Peter 1:20 The Son of God always existed and it was always known that He would be the Redeemer of mankind.*

This is very profound because it ties into not only the Lord's Prayer, but also into all the passages on patience as presented throughout these prophecies and throughout scripture. We are facing here on earth a way for God to prove our faithfulness not only to Him, but also against the evil opposition we face from the devil. Here I am led to refer to the sickness of Job. We see this in the conversation between God and Satan the explanation for all the tribulations which we all face. Satan is challenging the ability of God's plan to be successful.

> **JOB 2:2-10 AMPLIFIED BIBLE (AMP)**
> [2] *The Lord said to Satan, "From where have you come?" Then Satan answered the Lord, "From roaming around on the earth and from walking around on it."*
> [3] *The Lord said to Satan, "Have you considered and reflected on My servant Job? For there is none like him on the earth, a blameless and upright man, one who fears God [with reverence] and abstains from and turns away from evil [because he honors God]. And still he maintains and holds tightly to his integrity, although you incited Me against him to destroy him without cause."*
> [4] *Satan answered the Lord, "[a]Skin for skin! Yes, a man will give all he has for his life.*

> *⁵ But put forth Your hand now, and touch his bone and his flesh [and severely afflict him]; and he will curse You to Your face."*
> *⁶ So the Lord said to Satan, "Behold, he is in your hand, only spare his life."*
> *⁷ So Satan departed from the presence of the Lord and struck Job with loathsome boils and agonizingly painful sores from the sole of his foot to the crown of his head.*
> *⁸ And Job took a piece of broken pottery with which to scrape himself, and he sat [down] among the ashes (rubbish heaps).*
> *⁹ Then his wife said to him, "Do you still cling to your integrity [and your faith and trust in God, without blaming Him]? Curse God and die!"*
> *¹⁰ But he said to her, "You speak as one of the [spiritually] foolish women speaks [ignorant and oblivious to God's will]. Shall we indeed accept [only] good from God and not [also] accept adversity and disaster?" In [spite of] all this Job did not sin with [words from] his lips.*
>
> Footnotes:
> Job 2:4 This probably refers to a trade of one animal skin for another, but even so its application here is unclear. One possibility is that according to Satan, Job would be willing to give up his wife (his remaining loved one) to save his own life, thus surrendering his integrity (v 3). Another is that Satan is hypothetically offering to give up his own life if Job is actually willing to die for his integrity. In any case, this is a bluff on Satan's part, probably to make what he really wants (v 5) appear less drastic.

Yes, Satan has to have permission from God to bring temptations. which can include trials of sickness and other devices which he can use to test our faithfulness. God sets the limits on what Satan can do to us. This is a proof that the work of the Holy Spirit in us can be permanent and God's choice of us, as His, is not a mistake. God is showing to Satan that His righteous people are stronger than him. God is showing the righteous with the Holy Spirit have power over evil.

The Spirit has further opened my understanding of why the presentation of Job's temptation is so important. From the very beginning the devil has challenged God, especially His choice of how we could gain salvation. The devil takes every opportunity to try to prove himself superior to God. The devil's plan is to force us into submission or into failure, but the plan of God is just the opposite of this. God's plan is salvation based on the work of Jesus in us after receiving our permission and agreeing to allow Him to place the principles of God in us. The result is that we are the proof that the wisdom of God is greater than that of the devil. So, we are the proof of the pudding, so to speak. Therefore, as we successfully overcome temptation, we glorify God by demonstrating that His wisdom and power are ultimate and that none other but Him is supreme.

In each of these prophecies we see God is addressing the message to those who are willing to receive His message. None are being forced to accept it, as in the devil's plan. Those **(who have ears to hear)** is indicative of the message He extends to us all. If we are willing to receive it, we will gain the intent of this message. He is not forcing anyone to accept His invitation. It is our choice. It is by our choice we are condemned, not by His. It is because of His love He accepts our choice of either eternal life or eternal death. His love demands that justice be delivered to the rebellious so that the innocent can be avenged for the wrongs which they have suffered. This is the patience which we are called to have. In the end, all things will be made right according to God's just judgement, which is always administered in love.

Summary

Even though this prophecy is not very long, it carries such power. In this I find the answer to something which I have struggled with all my Christian life which is, why bad things happen to good people? I now have an answer to question.

Just as the church at Smyrna, this was a group of mature Christians. They also been transformed, just as the Pentecost Saints, with a spirit modeled after Jesus. He was able to tell them things in a way that baby Christians could not understand. They had received the strength only Godly love can provide. The words, Jesus spoke for them to bring glory and honor to God. They knew, without a doubt, that they had all of the power of the Godhead in them and they knew even death could not defeat the ultimate purpose of Jesus, which is to provide us eternal life and allow His plan to be fulfilled in them. They, just as the church at Smyrna, knew that their garments had been washed by the blood of the lamb and they could stand before God in confidence knowing they would hear the words "well done my good and faithful servants". Wouldn't we all desire to hear these words when we stand before God for final judgement?

MATTHEW 25:20-22 KING JAMES VERSION (KJV)
[20] And so he that had received five talents came and brought other five talents, saying, Lord, thou deliveredst unto me five talents: behold, I have gained beside them five talents more.
[21] His lord said unto him, Well done, thou good and faithful servant: thou hast been faithful over a few things, I will make thee ruler over many things: enter thou into the joy of thy lord.
[22] He also that had received two talents came and said, Lord, thou deliveredst unto me two talents: behold, I have gained two other talents beside them.

What are we to gain from this portion of this prophecy?

1. Here we see that God is demonstrating through our faithfulness that His wisdom is above that of His greatest adversary, the devil.
2. The trials we face are presented to all. Yet they are more than a thorn in our side. They are for the glory of God.
3. Each successful overcoming of a trial is a representation to the devil and all opposition to God that the wisdom of God is supreme and cannot be frustrated.
4. All Christians will not have to face temptations but we have an audience with God who provides a way around these.
5. As stated before, He stands with us in all trials.
6. Trials are proof that God is right. He will provide the strength we need to overcome them. Trials will come in many forms so we need to be equipped to handle them.
7. When we become mature Christians Jesus can talk to us as adults not as babes constantly having to repent.
8. Jesus is in control. It is Jesus and only Jesus who has control over salvation and entry into eternal life. No one but Him can prevent this. It is He who judges when and how the way is opened or closed. He sets the conditions, no one else.
9. All will have this open opportunity. It up to us to accept the offer or not.
10. When we are truly converted and accepted, and been transformed into duplicating the Love of God, we will have the

courage needed to face anything and that as mature Christians we will not fear any circumstance which stands before us.
11. Understand that perfect love within us from the Godhead is our shield against all situations which the devil can toss at us.

Chapter 9

Prophecy to the Church of the Laodiceans

REVELATION 3:14-22 KING JAMES VERSION (KJV)
14 And unto the angel of the Church of the Laodiceans write; These things saith the Amen, the faithful and true witness, the beginning of the creation of God;
15 I know thy works, that thou art neither cold nor hot: I would thou wert cold or hot.
16 So then because thou art lukewarm, and neither cold nor hot, I will spue thee out of my mouth.
17 Because thou sayest, I am rich, and increased with goods, and have need of nothing; and knowest not that thou art wretched, and miserable, and poor, and blind, and naked:
18 I counsel thee to buy of me gold tried in the fire, that thou mayest be rich; and white raiment, that thou mayest be clothed, and that the shame of thy nakedness do not appear; and anoint thine eyes with eyesalve, that thou mayest see.
19 As many as I love, I rebuke and chasten: be zealous therefore, and repent.
20 Behold, I stand at the door, and knock: if any man hear my voice, and open the door, I will come in to him, and will sup with him, and he with me.
21 To him that overcometh will I grant to sit with me in my throne, even as I also overcame, and am set down with my Father in his throne.
22 He that hath an ear, let him hear what the Spirit saith unto the Churches.

Here again Jesus addresses another group with plain language. In doing this He is demonstrating that He does not want the message being presented to be misunderstood. He starts with the fact that He is truthful and they can count on what He is saying as the absolute truth as and He has the final say so in their case.

He then tells them fact that the things they have been doing show no real commitment. He identifies that they are in the world trying to conform to this life. The statement, that their works are neither hot not cold, indicates they were not performing righteous works. This is exemplified in the parable of the talents as the person who hid his gift rather than using it in a way which would gain something useful.

MATTHEW 25:14-40 KING JAMES VERSION (KJV)
14 For the kingdom of heaven is as a man travelling into a far country, who called his own servants, and delivered unto them his goods.
15 And unto one he gave five talents, to another two, and to another one; to every man according to his several ability; and straightway took his journey.
16 Then he that had received the five talents went and traded with the same, and made them other five talents.
17 And likewise he that had received two, he also gained other two.
18 But he that had received one went and digged in the earth, and hid his lord's money.
19 After a long time the lord of those servants cometh, and reckoneth with them.
20 And so he that had received five talents came and brought other five talents, saying, Lord, thou deliveredst unto me five talents: behold, I have gained beside them five talents more.
21 His lord said unto him, Well done, thou good and faithful servant: thou hast been faithful over a few things, I will make thee ruler over many things: enter thou into the joy of thy lord.
22 He also that had received two talents came and said, Lord, thou deliveredst unto me two talents: behold, I have gained two other talents beside them.
23 His lord said unto him, Well done, good and faithful servant; thou hast been faithful over a few things, I will make thee ruler over many things: enter thou into the joy of thy lord.
24 Then he which had received the one talent came and said, Lord, I knew thee that thou art an hard man, reaping where thou hast not sown, and gathering where thou hast not strawed:

25 And I was afraid, and went and hid thy talent in the earth: lo, there thou hast that is thine.
26 His lord answered and said unto him, Thou wicked and slothful servant, thou knewest that I reap where I sowed not, and gather where I have not strawed:
27 Thou oughtest therefore to have put my money to the exchangers, and then at my coming I should have received mine own with usury.
28 Take therefore the talent from him, and give it unto him which hath ten talents.
29 For unto every one that hath shall be given, and he shall have abundance: but from him that hath not shall be taken away even that which he hath.
30 And cast ye the unprofitable servant into outer darkness: there shall be weeping and gnashing of teeth.
31 When the Son of man shall come in his glory, and all the holy angels with him, then shall he sit upon the throne of his glory:
32 And before him shall be gathered all nations: and he shall separate them one from another, as a shepherd divideth his sheep from the goats:
33 And he shall set the sheep on his right hand, but the goats on the left.
34 Then shall the King say unto them on his right hand, Come, ye blessed of my Father, inherit the kingdom prepared for you from the foundation of the world:
35 For I was an hungred, and ye gave me meat: I was thirsty, and ye gave me drink: I was a stranger, and ye took me in:
36 Naked, and ye clothed me: I was sick, and ye visited me: I was in prison, and ye came unto me.
37 Then shall the righteous answer him, saying, Lord, when saw we thee an hungred, and fed thee? or thirsty, and gave thee drink?
38 When saw we thee a stranger, and took thee in? or naked, and clothed thee?
39 Or when saw we thee sick, or in prison, and came unto thee?
40 And the King shall answer and say unto them, Verily I say unto you, Inasmuch as ye have done it unto one of the least of these my brethren, ye have done it unto me.

He states they were comfortable and satisfied in that they had more than what was sufficient, (unlike the Church at Smyrna which was poor in worldly goods). Like many today, they followed their lustful desires and satisfaction for possessions and considered this as acceptance of themselves and their lifestyle. Christ told them their wealth in worldly possessions was not the goal with which they needed to find satisfaction. Earthly wealth is not His objective. Jesus wants a people who see love of God and love of their fellow man as the desirable result of His ministry. He reverses the statement told to the Church of Smyrna. He tells them though they are comfortable in the possessions of this life, but they were poor in the things which count. This is made obvious by comparing them with the Church at Smyrna which was faithful in receiving the rejuvenating work of Jesus, but lacked worldly possessions. Smyrna was poor but rich. The Laodiceans were rich but poor. Here we see Jesus' view of the prosperity message many are spouting today. It was not wrong that they were prosperous. What was wrong was they hoarded what they had for use on their own lusts to the demise of their brothers and sisters unlike the church at Smyrna. Smyrna didn't have much but evidently, they used what they had for the good of all. I am led to repeat a scripture used in the review of the prophecy to the Church at Smyrna.

> *MATTHEW 6:1-25 KING JAMES VERSION (KJV)*
> *¹ Take heed that ye do not your alms before men, to be seen of them: otherwise ye have no reward of your Father which is in heaven.*
> *² Therefore when thou doest thine alms, do not sound a trumpet before thee, as the hypocrites do in the synagogues and in the streets, that they may have glory of men. Verily I say unto you, They have their reward.*
> *³ But when thou doest alms, let not thy left hand know what thy right hand doeth:*
> *⁴ That thine alms may be in secret: and thy Father which seeth in secret himself shall reward thee openly.*
> *⁵ And when thou prayest, thou shalt not be as the hypocrites are: for they love to pray standing in the synagogues and in the corners of the streets, that they may be seen of men. Verily I say unto you, They have their reward.*
> *⁶ But thou, when thou prayest, enter into thy closet, and when thou hast shut thy door, pray to thy Father which is in secret; and thy Father which seeth in secret shall reward thee openly.*
> *⁷ But when ye pray, use not vain repetitions, as the heathen do: for they think that they shall be heard for their much speaking.*

⁸ Be not ye therefore like unto them: for your Father knoweth what things ye have need of, before ye ask him.
⁹ After this manner therefore pray ye: Our Father which art in heaven, Hallowed be thy name.
¹⁰ Thy kingdom come, Thy will be done in earth, as it is in heaven.
¹¹ Give us this day our daily bread.
¹² And forgive us our debts, as we forgive our debtors.
¹³ And lead us not into temptation, but deliver us from evil: For thine is the kingdom, and the power, and the glory, for ever. Amen.
¹⁴ For if ye forgive men their trespasses, your heavenly Father will also forgive you:
¹⁵ But if ye forgive not men their trespasses, neither will your Father forgive your trespasses.
¹⁶ Moreover when ye fast, be not, as the hypocrites, of a sad countenance: for they disfigure their faces, that they may appear unto men to fast. Verily I say unto you, They have their reward.
¹⁷ But thou, when thou fastest, anoint thine head, and wash thy face;
¹⁸ That thou appear not unto men to fast, but unto thy Father which is in secret: and thy Father, which seeth in secret, shall reward thee openly.
¹⁹ Lay not up for yourselves treasures upon earth, where moth and rust doth corrupt, and where thieves break through and steal:
²⁰ But lay up for yourselves treasures in heaven, where neither moth nor rust doth corrupt, and where thieves do not break through nor steal:
²¹ For where your treasure is, there will your heart be also.
²² The light of the body is the eye: if therefore thine eye be single, thy whole body shall be full of light.
²³ But if thine eye be evil, thy whole body shall be full of darkness. If therefore the light that is in thee be darkness, how great is that darkness!
²⁴ No man can serve two masters: for either he will hate the one, and love the other; or else he will hold to the one, and despise the other. Ye cannot serve God and mammon.
²⁵ Therefore I say unto you, Take no thought for your life, what ye shall eat, or what ye shall drink; nor yet for your body, what ye shall put on. Is not the life more than meat, and the body than raiment?

Here again, He is emphasizing that what was demonstrated by those in the Church formed at Pentecost holds true for all time. The Laodiceans were not demonstrating a transformed heart and mind because they choose possessing and the good life above the wok of the Holy Spirit which wanted them to love God above all else and to love brothers and sisters as themselves. They were letting the lust of their hearts rule and not the transforming work of the Holy Spirit. Here is a message for the Church today. The way we open our wallets indicates the depth of what we believe. The FBI states by looking into how a person spends his or her money, they can tell you what the person believes. It is how and what we spend our money on which indicates where our heart lies. They were trying to hide the true intent of using the goods and wealth they had for personal gain, consuming it on their lusts and not for the glory of God nor for the benefit of others.

I find I have lived as those of the Church of Laodicea. I have squandered my living on my lustful desires and have missed an opportunity to live in a way which glorifies God. I now live a life which is minimal in comparison to the way He has desired. Thanks be to God for the forgiveness I have found in Jesus Christ. I had followed the American dream which is get as much as you can accumulate to outdo the guy next door. Or to use a cliché I was trying to keep up with the Jones'.

He told them that the reason they are being pointed out here is because He still loves them. He is always concerned with our choices and the way we live and what we demonstrate to the world.

Let's not overlook the fact that we have a time limit which is staring us in the face. With that in mind, He encourages them to be zealous in responding to the call for them to repent. He wants them to become excited and to place this as the first priority in life. Our response should be a "now, not later" situation for none have a clue of when it will be too late to make our mark for Him here on earth. He tells them that if they don't wake up and continue to lulled into unresponsiveness, that He will come at a time at when they are not ready, unexpectedly. You see, we are all to keep watch for our hour is not promised nor is the time going to be apparent unless we keep our spiritual eyes on Him.

Jesus also points to the fact that He will chasten or issue a wakeup call to provide us guidance needed to stay on track. That should be the role of any parent who loves their children. When we see our children going wrong or entering a dangerous situation, we warn them of the danger and try to get them turned around. I am led to relate to you an incident which occurred in Tulsa a couple of weeks ago. There was a woman who had two youngsters. Their ages were two and three years old. She was on drugs and had let the kids wander off. One of the other family members reported the kids missing. In a tv interview, the mother was asked about the kids and why she didn't watch over them. She stated that she never wanted them in the first place and that she didn't care about them. A few days later the kids were found dead in a creek. Jesus is not that way. He loves us enough to warn us and to try to prevent us from dying an unjust death. It is not the death of the body which is His major concern but the second death which is the death of the spirit which is eternal punishment and from which there is no return. He desires that none should perish if they will accept His offer of forgiveness.

Summary

It is not difficult to identify the eternal truths provided here. Let's recap them:
1. The word of God is true and does not change.
2. He is displeased with those who ignore the call to love as He loves and to love others in the same way.
3. He is interested in how we have responded to the transforming work of the Holy Spirit and how we have accepted it and put it to use in our lives.
4. He is always offering an opportunity for us to repent. As is pointed out here, He indicates we need to respond promptly because we are limited in the time which we have to respond.
5. Lust of possessions is a major cause of those in the Church being misled into a so-so attitude. They become satisfied with their wealth and become blind to the work of the Holy Spirit.
6. Just being identified as part of the Church seemed to satisfy them. They were not heeding the call to be ever responsive to the work of the Spirit, which provides the incentive needed to perform the work we are called to, which is spreading the gospel (building the kingdom here on earth).

7. He emphasizes that we should not be lulled to sleep by using the standards of this life. We are to seek first His righteousness and then we will have what is needful for us in this life.
8. Jesus wants to rescue us from ourselves. He wants us to not sin unto the second death but to enjoy living with Him in eternal bliss.

CHAPTER 10

Jesus, His Closing Statement

I have been led to provide a summary here. There are definite patterns which we can identify in these prophecies. So here they are.
1. Jesus presents himself to each Church using attributes emphasizing how He wants them to perceive Him.
2. Please note that Jesus acts out of His love for them because it is His desire that none perish.
3. In each one He recognizes the works which they are producing. When they are performing works as ordained by God there is no need for Him to provide rebukes or correction.
4. In Churches which are not providing works which are God ordained He calls for repentance.
5. In Churches where there are members or others which have held on to sinful conduct or where there are false prophets, He calls for repentance and for us to recognize this sin and expose it.
6. He points to punishment being required if they do not repent.
7. He always has a faithful group in each of His Churches.
8. He provides insight into the fact that those who are doing as He has ordained will receive the rewards He promised.
9. He declares the unpardonable sin; those who have come to a full knowledge of Him and then turn away will go into the lake of fire and no longer can receive forgiveness. This is the second death.

10. He provides insight that each Church has an ultimate purpose. That is to glorify God in all that they do and how they have either strayed from this or have complied to this plan.
11. He informs everyone they can expect trials and tribulation all of which is for the glory of God.
12. He says they need to practice patience which is holding on to the promises of God and the ultimate reward which is eternal life.
13. Lastly, He provides the fact that He is in constant support and He is there to support them as needed.
14. As always, He emphasizes no one is forced to respond to Him. This is stated in each prophecy by the statement He makes; "those who have ears to hear let him hear what the spirit has to say to the Churches".
15. We also find two groups of mature saints which had been transformed into the image of Christ which could handle the meat of the word, without reservation, which is where we should be seeking to duplicate.

Summary

There will be more to be added to this in Part 2 but I was led to end with this part of this prophecy as a closing and as an introduction to the next book, Part 2.

1. Now the wrap up He provides.

REVELATION 22:1-21 KING JAMES VERSION (KJV)
¹ And he shewed me a pure river of water of life, clear as crystal, proceeding out of the throne of God and of the Lamb.

² In the midst of the street of it, and on either side of the river, was there the tree of life, which bare twelve manner of fruits, and yielded her fruit every month: and the leaves of the tree were for the healing of the nations.

³ And there shall be no more curse: but the throne of God and of the Lamb shall be in it; and his servants shall serve him:

⁴ And they shall see his face; and his name shall be in their foreheads.

⁵ And there shall be no night there; and they need no candle, neither light of the sun; for the Lord God giveth them light: and they shall reign for ever and ever.

⁶ And he said unto me, These sayings are faithful and true: and the Lord God of the holy prophets sent his angel to shew unto his servants the things which must shortly be done.

⁷ Behold, I come quickly: blessed is he that keepeth the sayings of the prophecy of this book.

⁸ And I John saw these things, and heard them. And when I had heard and seen, I fell down to worship before the feet of the angel which shewed me these things.

⁹ Then saith he unto me, See thou do it not: for I am thy fellowservant, and of thy brethren the prophets, and of them which keep the sayings of this book: worship God.

¹⁰ And he saith unto me, Seal not the sayings of the prophecy of this book: for the time is at hand.

¹¹ He that is unjust, let him be unjust still: and he which is filthy, let him be filthy still: and he that is righteous, let him be righteous still: and he that is holy, let him be holy still.

¹² And, behold, I come quickly; and my reward is with me, to give every man according as his work shall be.

¹³ I am Alpha and Omega, the beginning and the end, the first and the last.

¹⁴ Blessed are they that do his commandments, that they may have right to the tree of life, and may enter in through the gates into the city.

¹⁵ For without are dogs, and sorcerers, and whoremongers, and murderers, and idolaters, and whosoever loveth and maketh a lie.

¹⁶ I Jesus have sent mine angel to testify unto you these things in the Churches. I am the root and the offspring of David, and the bright and morning star.

¹⁷ And the Spirit and the bride say, Come. And let him that heareth say, Come. And let him that is athirst come. And whosoever will, let him take the water of life freely.

¹⁸ For I testify unto every man that heareth the words of the prophecy of this book, If any man shall add unto these things, God shall add unto him the plagues that are written in this book:

¹⁹ And if any man shall take away from the words of the book of this prophecy, God shall take away his part out of the book of life, and out of the holy city, and from the things which are written in this book.

²⁰ He which testifieth these things saith, Surely I come quickly. Amen. Even so, come, Lord Jesus.

²¹ The grace of our Lord Jesus Christ be with you all. Amen.

Post Script

I would like to ask a favor of you. I would appreciate it if you would provide an honest evaluation of this book and post it on my Facebook page for this book and if you have an Amzon.com account please add it there also. If you wish I would also like your permission to share your comments with others.

Appendix

Scripture References

COPYRIGHT	II
TABLE OF CONTENTS	III
REVELATION 1:18-19 KING JAMES VERSION (KJV)	V
EZEKIEL 12:1-3 AMPLIFIED BIBLE (AMP)	V
LUKE 14:34-35 KING JAMES VERSION (KJV)	V
LEVITICUS 24:3-4 AMPLIFIED BIBLE (AMP)	V
CHAPTER 1. INTRODUCTION TO THE PROPHECY TO THE SEVEN CHURCHES	**1**
MATTHEW 6:30-34 KING JAMES VERSION (KJV)	2
REVELATION 1:10-20 KING JAMES VERSION (KJV)	3
1 JOHN 3:1-10 AMPLIFIED BIBLE	5
EXODUS 30:26-28 KING JAMES VERSION (KJV)	6
EXODUS 35:13-15 KING JAMES VERSION (KJV)	6
LEVITICUS 24:3-4 AMPLIFIED BIBLE (AMP)	6
MATTHEW 5:14-16 KING JAMES VERSION (KJV)	7
EXODUS 27:19-21 AMPLIFIED BIBLE	8
MATTHEW 25:2-10 KING JAMES VERSION (KJV)	8
1 CORINTHIANS 12:27-29 KING JAMES VERSION (KJV)	9
1 TIMOTHY 3:1-15 KING JAMES VERSION (KJV)	9
EPHESIANS 4:1-30 KING JAMES VERSION (KJV).	10
ACTS 2:38-40 KING JAMES VERSION (KJV)	12
EPHESIANS 5:26-28 AMPLIFIED BIBLE	12
SUMMARY	13
CHAPTER 2. THE CHURCH JESUS BUILT AT PENTECOST	**15**
ACTS 2:2-47 KING JAMES VERSION (KJV)	17
GALATIANS 3:27-29 AMPLIFIED BIBLE (AMP)	20
1 CORINTHIANS 2:14-16 AMPLIFIED BIBLE (AMP)	20
1 CORINTHIANS 5:12-13 AMPLIFIED BIBLE (AMP)	20
1 CORINTHIANS 14:20-33 KING JAMES VERSION (KJV)	21
LUKE 4:14-21 KING JAMES VERSION (KJV)	22
1 CORINTHIANS 15:10-25 KING JAMES VERSION (KJV)	23
1 CORINTHIANS 15:31-50 KING JAMES VERSION (KJV)	23

Acts 5:1-15 Amplified Bible (AMP)	26
Ephesians 4:17-30 Amplified Bible (AMP)	28
Summary	29
CHAPTER 3. PROPHECY TO THE CHURCH OF EPHESUS	**31**
Revelation 2:1-7 King James Version (KJV)	31
Acts 11:1-18 King James Version (KJV)	32
Ephesians 4:17-32 Amplified Bible (AMP)	34
Summary	38
Matthew 7:10-16 King James Version (KJV)	38
2 Timothy 4:2-4 King James Version	39
Revelation 2:7 King James Version (KJV)	40
CHAPTER 4. PROPHECY TO THE CHURCH IN SMYRNA	**41**
Revelation 2:8-11 King James Version (KJV)	41
1 Corinthians 10:2-4 King James Version (KJV)	41
2 Corinthians 3:17-18 King James Version (KJV)	42
2 Corinthians 4:12-14 King James Version (KJV)	42
Psalm 23:1-6 King James Version (KJV)	43
Matthew 10:37-39 King James Version (KJV)	44
Luke 14:26-28 Amplified Bible (AMP)	44
Matthew 6:1-25 King James Version (KJV)	45
Jeremiah 10:12-14 King James Version (KJV)	48
Jeremiah 10:12-14 Amplified Bible (AMP)	48
Summary	50
John 9:1-38 King James Version (KJV)	52
1 Chronicles 16:33-35 King James Version (KJV)	54
CHAPTER 5. PROPHECY TO THE CHURCH IN PERGAMOS	**57**
Revelation 2:12-17 King James Version (KJV)	57
Acts 15:15-33 King James Version (KJV)	58
Matthew 6:23-25 King James Version (KJV)	59
Ephesians 4:17-32 King James Version (KJV)	60
1 Corinthians 15:31-37 Amplified Bible (AMP)	61
Genesis 17:4-6 Amplified Bible (AMP)	62
Genesis 17:14-16 King James Version (KJV)	63
Genesis 32:24-32 King James Version (KJV)	63
Summary	64
CHAPTER 6. PROPHECY TO THE CHURCH IN THYATIRA	**67**
Revelation 2:18-29 King James Version (KJV)	67
1 Corinthians 13:2-13 King James Version (KJV)	69
Romans 12:1-3 King James Version (KJV)	71
Titus 2:11-15 King James Version (KJV)	71
Acts 8:1-25 King James Version (KJV)	72

EXODUS 7:9-12 KING JAMES VERSION (KJV) 74
ACTS 13:5-7 KING JAMES VERSION (KJV) 74
2 CHRONICLES 5:10-14 KING JAMES VERSION (KJV) 76
PSALM 117:1-2 KING JAMES VERSION (KJV) 76
MATTHEW 10:21-23 AMPLIFIED BIBLE (KJV) 77
2 TIMOTHY 4:2-4 KING JAMES VERSION (KJV) 78
2 CHRONICLES 21:10-17 KING JAMES VERSION (KJV) 79
EZEKIEL 16:28-30 KING JAMES VERSION (KJV) 80
1 CORINTHIANS 10:5-15 KING JAMES VERSION (KJV) 81
SUMMARY 82

CHAPTER 7.   PROPHECY TO THE CHURCH IN SARDIS   85
REVELATION 3:1-6 KING JAMES VERSION (KJV) 85
LUKE 21:33-35 AMPLIFIED BIBLE 86
SECTION 76:4A-4F DOCTRINE & COVENANTS....................... 87
SUMMARY... 88

CHAPTER 8.   PROPHECY TO THE CHURCH IN PHILADELPHIA
                                                                                    91
REVELATION 3:7-13 KING JAMES VERSION (KJV) 91
JAMES 1:1-3 KING JAMES VERSION (KJV) 94
JAMES 1:13-15 KING JAMES VERSION (KJV) 94
1 PETER 1:3-25 AMPLIFIED BIBLE (AMP) 94
JOB 2:2-10 AMPLIFIED BIBLE (AMP) 96
SUMMARY 98
MATTHEW 25:20-22 KING JAMES VERSION (KJV) 99

CHAPTER 9.   PROPHECY TO THE CHURCH OF THE LAODICEANS
                                                                                    101
REVELATION 3:14-22 KING JAMES VERSION (KJV) 101
MATTHEW 25:14-40 KING JAMES VERSION (KJV) 102
MATTHEW 6:1-25 KING JAMES VERSION (KJV) 104
SUMMARY 107

CHAPTER 10.   JESUS, HIS CLOSING STATEMENT   109
SUMMARY 110
REVELATION 22:1-21 KING JAMES VERSION (KJV) 110

POST SCRIPT   **113**
APPENDIX   **114**
SCRIPTURE REFERENCES   **115**
ABOUT THE AUTHOR   **118**

About the Author

OR SCRIBE (AS I SEE IT)

Lorenzo Hill and his wife Clotilde right after marriage, 1969

Lorenzo Hill and his wife Clotilde after 49 years, 2018
We have now been married 52 years As of April 2020

Lorenzo Hill has served in the ministry of the Community of Christ (formerly The Reorganized Church of Jesus Christ Of Latter Day Saints) since 1976, when he was ordained a priest. Throughout his ministry, he has been a self-supporting minister. He has served in his current office of Evangelist since 1988 and continues to be very active in ministry, serving in various roles of leadership and other roles in which he is called to serve. His passion has been providing guidance to youth. He had to sadly stop this part of his ministry for health reasons. He provides ongoing ministry through his commitment to spreading word in preaching and bringing ministry to the sick in soul and body.

Lorenzo was raised in St. Louis Missouri and resided there until he received his Bachelor of Science degree in Chemical Engineering in 1970 from the University of Missouri at Rolla (currently known as the Missouri School of Science and Technology). He is a registered retired professional engineer. He has worked in the petroleum industry since he graduated from college and has retired twice. Needless to say, he has moved around quite a bit. He has been blessed to be able to see many other countries because of his employment and for pleasure. The Holy Spirit has used this to open his eyes to the suffering that many experiences in this life due to governmental policies and personal lifestyles.

He has been married to his wife, Clotilde for 51 years. She has been his constant support in all his endeavors. They have three children: two daughters Alicia Renee Hill, Reynada Charlese Robinson, and one son, Jared Lorenzo Hill.

Although he has taken many post graduate courses in both engineering and ministry, Lorenzo chose not to pursue an advanced degree. He has written numerous technical reports and technical texts for the training and instruction of engineers and construction inspectors. All of these works, however, were prepared for either clients or for internal company use and as such, were not issued as external publications.

He has been inspired to publish four books. These books are titled:
Formulas In The Scripture: E =MC2
And
What God Intends for Us in His Commandments
And
Eternal Life

And this book
What God is Saying in the Book of Revelation

These works are currently in print and can be purchased on Amazon.com in paperback or e-book format.

If there is one way to express His walk with Christ there are some words from a hymn in our Church entitled Admonition. These are as follows:

"Grace waits upon the souls who try"

As Paul states I am not perfect yet, but I strive for the high calling of Christ Jesus and await the transformation to be like Him in all ways. Thanks to my wife and daughters for proof reading these works. Praise be to God for His inspiring spirit, enlightenment and encouragement. It is by God's grace I have been allowed to present His intent and purposes in these books so that we may all know the truth of the Gospel.

www.ingramcontent.com/pod-product-compliance
Lightning Source LLC
LaVergne TN
LVHW051503070426
835507LV00022B/2900